DOOMSDAY CULTS

DOOMSDAY CULTS

THE DEVIL'S HOSTAGES

ALAN R. WARREN

ALAN R. WARREN

COPYRIGHT

DOOMSDAY CULTS: The Devils Hostages
Written by ALAN R. WARREN

Published in Canada

This is a work of nonfiction. No names have been changed, no characters invented, no events fabricated.

Cover design, formatting, layout, and editing by Evening Sky Publishing Services

BOOK DESCRIPTION

Jim Jones convinced his 1000 followers they would all have to commit suicide now that he was going to die. Shoko Asahara convinced his followers to release a weapon of mass destruction, the deadly sarin gas, on a Tokyo subway, killing 13 people and harming countless others. The Order of the Solar Temple cult leaders convinced the rich and famous, including Princess Grace of Monaco, to join their ranks. Later, they also convinced them that to be reborn on the better planet, Sirius, they had to die a fiery death here on Earth. Charles Manson convinced his followers to kill, in an attempt to incite an apocalyptic race war. Rod Ferrell convinced his followers that he was a 500-year-old Vampire, and it was okay to drink each other's blood. The Children of God, a.k.a. The Family International, continue to believe they are the end times messenger for Jesus, and so does their 10,000+ membership.

These are a few of the doomsday cults examined in this book by bestselling author Alan R. Warren. Its focus will be on the cults whose destructive behavior was due in large part to their apocalyptic beliefs or doomsday movements.

Why did these massacres happen, and how did these people get so brainwashed? When we hear about these cults, we all wonder the same things, including who is to blame? We also could ask what then is the difference between a small group of people that gave themselves over to one person who believed they were the son of God and a cult?

This book in no way criticizes believing in God. Rather, it examines how a social movement grows into a full religion and when it does not. How does a movement become a religion? And what makes the accepted existing religions such as Christianity, Judaism, Islam, and Hinduism stand above groups such as the Branch Davidians or Heaven's Gate?

CONTENTS

INTRODUCTION

"Let's Go to Doctor everything's going to be alright, make everything go wrong" - Prince

The only way I can get through writing about such dreadful subjects is by countering it with some fitting dance music. Like what Prince says,

"Dearly beloved, we have gathered here today to get through this thing called life."

After all, life is what it's all about.

MY EXPERIENCE WITH RELIGION

If you have not been raised in a specific Orthodoxy (i.e., brought up in a religion), then you probably grew up similar to how I did. My family always said we were Christian when asked, but didn't attend any church services. My Sunday Service was playing outside with my dog and eating a popsicle.

When I began school, the question "Your family is Christian, right?" came up. My first-grade teacher asked me as part of her administration work, and I answered her with an enthusiastic, "Yes!" Looking back, I don't know why I was so excited. But how could I not be happy? Everyone else in the classroom was answering yes to the same question and seemed to be joyous about it too. Power of persuasion, perhaps?

Being a Christian appeared to be great. I was liked because of it, my teachers were happy that I was a one, we had a great life, and I never had to do anything extra to be one, so why not? It wasn't until junior high that I heard anything to the contrary. One day, another student told me that I was going to go to hell. Of course, I answered, "Yeah, why would I do that? I'm a Christian." She snapped back, sternly, "Because you haven't been baptized."

I was frozen. What did it mean to be 'baptized?' I became immediately silent and never spoke another word to her. Don't take that the wrong way. It's not like I was hurt; I was just processing what information she gave me and needed time to do that. Remember, I'm autistic, and I'm told that we are not comfortable sharing our feelings, especially in public. But I differ in this way.

I needed more information; I was going to ask for my

mother's perspective on baptism. Later that afternoon, when I arrived home from school, my mother was not there. My older sister was, however, so I told her what had been said to me at school that day. My sister was around 16 years old, used marijuana like most kids of the time, listened to rock music, dated boys, and skipped school a lot. So, her response? She laughed, really hard, and told me that this girl who said that to me just needed to get laid. She also told me not to worry about the little b****. My sister wanted me to give her the name of the student so she could 'take care' of her. I didn't want that. Fighting was not in my nature, so I told my sister I didn't know it, but when I got it, I'd tell her.

The question lingered in my mind for several years, "Could I be a Christian if I wasn't baptized?"

Life moved on until I was college age when there was a new question,

"What are you looking for in life?" And even deeper still, "What does it all mean?"

These are questions we all face at one time or another. And sometimes these questions can lead us to great pain or disappointment: from the job, career, or lack thereof, perhaps the mate we chose, or some other superficial thing we're told we needed to be a good person. We began the search to find that, whatever 'that' was?

So, what to do?

Buy something! Yes, that's it! Retail therapy. We remember seeing a great advertisement on television, and this family bought a brand new car, and wow, there were all so happy and in love! So that' must be the right thing to do. We buy a car and are pretty excited about it. We get home, and the wife doesn't like the color, the kids spill their ice cream on the new seats, and our neighbor next door just bought the newer model.

Well, that didn't work! What now?

We look for something to numb the disappointment we are feeling. Quite often, it's some sort of substance like drugs, alcohol, sex, food, or anything that gives us a good feeling at the time of taking it. It's like wearing a cozy warm coat in winter. And everything feels fine. But when that substance wears off, we are back to where we started.

Upon more reflection, we think we have it all figured out! We'll go natural. We'll start eating the latest in holistic all-natural meatless meat. And join Bikram yoga. We hear he's the coolest guy and has excellent insight. We just need to borrow some money to pay for his $5,000 fee for weekend classes. We get the Bikram yoga mat, only $500, even though we sure it looks like the one we saw at Walmart last week for $30. But there's probably something very magical about Bikram's mat, and it might not work if we don't have it.

We find people that seem to have it all: money, fame, looks, health, and they're always happy. We start to dress like them, copy everything they do, go to the same concerts, and scream our heads off when they do. But then, it ends a little differently. The star gets old, not so nice looking anymore, their music or movies are out of touch, or they disappear, die in some vulgar out-of-the-way place, wearing women's panties, and so on.

Next up?

I got it! Maybe a new religion. But this time, take it seriously. Attend the classes, learn, and live the righteous way.

And that's how it starts.

LOSING MY RELIGION

Whenever someone asks me the question, “Do you believe in God?” I usually want to respond with, “Which God do you mean?” When I read a story about a person that nearly escaped death during a major catastrophe, and they claim, “God was protecting me.” Again, I want to ask them, “Which God?”

There have been so many gods worshipped throughout history. For example, the Vikings had Odin, Baldr, Freya, and Thor, to name a few. The ancient Egyptians, Greeks, and Romans were polytheistic (i.e., believing in several gods at once) as well. Zeus, Hera, and Poseidon were just a few of the Greek gods, and the other civilizations had their equivalent.

Many of the ancient civilizations thought their Gods were real, just as the followers of today’s religions do. They prayed to them, sacrificed animals to them, thanked them when things were good, and blamed them when things were bad.

How is it that we know now that these ancient people weren’t right?

It’s hard to believe that in the twentieth century, scientists predicted that belief in God would decrease to the fewest number of followers in the history of humanity. When, in fact, the opposite has occurred. Never in history has there been such a high percentage of the human population believing in some sort of God.

For me, now, life’s big question has moved to, “Which God do I believe in and follow?” There are plenty of choices out there. A quick search on the internet gave me more than 2,500 from which to choose! I don’t have the time to research all 2,500 to make my decision. I mean that literally since I'm already 57 years old.

Logically, the best way to choose would be to select the top 15 Gods of the day, since most of the others are just some sort of variation anyway, and research those. Jesus Christ has over 2 billion followers, Allah has 1.6 billion followers, Shiva, the most worshipped God of Hinduism, or Buddha, who claims not to be a God, but a way of worship that revolves around ethical conduct and inner purity.

There's also the popularity of the New Age spiritual movement that has returned stronger than ever before. New Age spirituality covers everything from Ghosts, after-life projects, Mediums speaking to our passed loved ones, witches, and even aliens from another planet, all taking the platform of 'religion.'

After all, it is the intellectual and spiritual quest to understand the universe and our place in it that is the fundamental reason for the search for God.

Why does the difference in people's choice in religions and beliefs create such hatred to the point of killing? The answer can be found in the contrast of why we think others believe in God. We don't just try to find reasons why one God is better than the other. It's much easier to talk about how some member of a particular religion misbehaves as the reason that their God can't be the 'right' God.

On a personal level, I found myself much more attracted to the spiritualist ideas and wanting to learn about that first. Probably because one of the first things I learned about spiritualist groups, was that they were open to anybody. It didn't matter about your race or your sexual orientation. It is more focused on our inner being. It is also easier to assimilate with my current lifestyle as it fits into the type of 'Christian' that I was.

The popularity in mediums, psychics, and UFO experiencers has led to a magical type of thinking in the general population. So much so, that it doesn't matter what science has proven. When it's up against how we emotionally feel about things, science will always have a hard time. Much of the paranormal world has no scientific data to support it, and we have to rely on what people claim. And some genuinely believe them. Emotions have a tremendous influence on that.

What is the mechanism by which a person comes to believe that any supreme being has orchestrated our entire lives? Right down to the finest detail of our thoughts. How is it we believe that a supreme being has created all events in our lives? Whether good and bad. These questions are always challenging to answer with logic.

The most common reasons people provide for their belief in a certain God or religion falls to the design argument and the beautiful complexities of the grand design of the world in which we all live. This would all have to be the result of the designer by using our spiritual senses.

People strive to find answers in stories and myths found in each of our histories and cultures. We search for patterns that our brains can recognize and follow, as they must be proof of a design created for us.

Like creation myths, most cultures have destruction and end of the world myths. And usually, redemption myths there to save us. We have quite an ego to think that everything was created just for us. But such is the basis of humanity. Even though science has given us viable alternatives to explain the universe, we still search for some sort of spiritual reason to answer our questions.

JESUS VS. CHARLES MANSON?

When the Roman Emperor, Constantine I, converted to Christianity in 312 A.D., it was a shock. Previous Emperors were outright hostile toward what they considered to be a cult, Christianity. At the time, Christians were a small group of people that followed a man who claimed to be the son of God, had healing powers, and died on the cross for people's sins. Even in today's standards, this sounds like a cult. And it most likely would be considered one.

For this reason, could Jesus have been the first 'Charles Manson' in history? Like during the summer of love in 1967, when Manson was only one of many gurus running around with a guitar, long hair, and preaching the message of love. Why did Manson rise above the rest? It's easier for us to find evidence and reason behind his actions, but because Jesus lived millennia ago, we don't have the proof.

Constantine's approval led to Yahweh being worshipped around the world today. At the time, though, there were several tribes with several Gods, but having the Roman Empire naming Christianity an official religion gave them protection the other groups didn't have.

Initially, Christians were considered atheists because they didn't believe in Jupiter or Neptune or any of the Roman Gods. Today, atheists are considered people that don't believe in any God at all. Most religious people today follow the God of the Jews, Yahweh. Both Christianity and Islam are offshoots of the ancient Jewish religion.

If you recall, the first part of the Christian Bible, The Old Testament, is purely Jewish. Also, the Muslim Quran is derived from the Jewish scriptures. All three of these religions are considered Abrahamic religions, as they all trace back to the patriarch, Abraham, who is regarded as the founder of the Jewish people.

All three of these religions are also considered monotheistic as they only have one God. Except for their devil-like character, Satan in Christianity and Shaytan in Islam, who has the power of a God and uses the forces of evil to wage constant war against the good people of God. It is an important distinction that not only do atheists not believe in a God such as Jesus, but they also do not believe in evil Gods such as Satan. Only religious people believe in Satan or Shaytan.

Do we honestly need God to be good people? In America, the actual Constitution says that "no religious test shall ever be required as a qualification to any office or public trust under the United States." Yet, it would seem that it's an essential requirement to hold office. This fact is significant in understanding the state of mind of the country. Even though the people chosen to lead the country make decisions on everything from finances, health, and legal matters, why would religion help make better decisions? It seems that the majority of the public think you need to believe in a higher power to be a good person.

SIMILARITIES BETWEEN CULTS AND RELIGIONS

What is the difference between a small group of people that gave themselves over to one person who believed they were the son of God and a cult? How do we determine the difference? What are our criteria for this subject?

Is it okay to believe in God? This question causes immense controversy, and people quickly get angry when trying to discuss the matter. I'm not trying to answer this question in this book. Instead, I am trying to examine how religion, as we know it today, ties into what we call cults, and to figure out if there is a difference. If so, then what is that difference? Where do we draw the line between the two of them?

When someone rises among the people as a religious leader, how do we discern if they are real or just about control? Do we, as a society, not allow such groups to grow? And are we better off or worse off for not allowing them to grow?

How does a movement become a religion that should be allowed to flourish? What makes the accepted existing religions such as Christianity, Judaism, Islam, and Hinduism stand above groups such as the Branch Davidians or Heaven's Gate?

Here are some similarities between cults and religions:

- ***Conspiracy Theories*** **-** A significant theme you'll find in both cults and religions is conspiracy theories and the arrogance that comes along with staunch believers of both. Some religions and cults will twist and bend science to suit their purpose or defend their conspiracy theory.

- ***Elements of Control*** - All of these groups are looking not only to fulfill the needs of their followers but to exploit them as well. As long as a leader and follower relationship exist in a group (i.e., a hierarchy), there will be an element of control. Sometimes the conditioning isn't so obvious; it can be more subtle. For example, if you are often told that to have sex is impure and a bad thing until marriage, by the time you get married, your feeling toward sex may be that it's dirty.
- ***Prophecies*** - Both established religions and doomsday cults recognize prophecies. Is this the time of the antiChrist? Are these the end times? Both are the most common questions we get coming from both types of groups. Why is it that the leader of the Christian religion is more believable than David Koresh? After all, we are all just humans, and in reality, none of us knows what happens after our deaths.
- ***Self-Glorification*** - A leader of a cult or church will sometimes call upon one of their followers while giving a sermon. By bringing the follower forward, it draws attention to that person and creates the illusion that the follower is important and exceptional. It supports their value to not only the church, but the world, and they feel heard. We tend to gravitate towards celebrities and people that speak in public, especially if they say things that we can relate

> to or with which we agree. Therefore, we feel closer to them and sometimes even think that we are friends with them.

Most leaders of the cults we will review here in this book appear to have been followers of quite a few conspiracy theories. Theories I consider to be conspiratorial, and the formula behind the thinking that hitches onto these theories are included. It becomes not so much what's in theory, but the formula that's written into them.

Also explained in this book is that sometimes the theory sold to a person is so convincing that a follower not only believes it but changes their entire lifestyle to become part of the plan. So even after the group leader is gone or proven wrong, some followers will continue to live out their lives, still believing in the teachings of that leader. This failure to accept the truth happens for a few reasons. One of which is the inability to admit the amount of time invested in the cult was wrong.

At this point, we will focus on the things that we know, rather than guessing. This book is not about ripping apart the personal beliefs of people, but rather to expand on our existing science and move forward. Yet, I can't help but wonder if I were to rewrite this book in 10 or 20 years from now, would any of the current religions then be considered just another doomsday cult.

I

RELIGION AND CULTS

"These children that come at you with knives – they are your children. You taught them. I didn't teach them. I just tried to help them stand up." - Charles Manson

1

CULTISM

The word "cult" comes from the Latin "cultus." which means 'to till or cultivate.' Of course, in old times, this was meant to cultivate favor with the Gods, through sacrifices, offerings, or by building giant statues to please them.

In modern times, a cult is broadly defined as a system of religious beliefs, where usually, the religion is regarded as unorthodox, and its group of followers has a great devotion to the person or idea.

There are three main characteristics of a cult:

- The group is led by a charismatic leader who is authoritarian and demands to be revered as a God-like figure;
- The group has some form of indoctrination program or thought reform (mind control) process;
- The members are being exploited - usually

financially, sexually, for labor, or some other sort of exploitation.

The problem with the word 'cult' is that in today's world, it has become a value judgment instead of a functional term. Every group or religion that has come before, and done something that is considered horrible, is called a cult. Every major religious leader or prophet can be regarded as a charismatic leader. A common statement within religious studies groups is that "cult plus time equals religion." In modern times, scholars refer to these cults as "New Religious Movements" or NRM.

The Roman Empire initially considered Judaism as a cult. Jesus was one of at least a dozen religious 'messiahs' during socially turbulent times. Many religions movements rose to help people get through life in those troubled times. Most of them were not trying to exploit their followers but to help them survive.

In the Middle East, we had religious movements such as Christianity, Manichaeism, Sunni Islam, Shia Islam, Yazidism, Ebionites, and Valentinian Gnosticism. In Europe, we saw Waldensians, Hussites, Christian Kabbalah, Familists, Hutterian Brethren, Albigensian, and Rosicrucianism as a backlash against institutional religions. In India, as a response to British colonialism, there was Sikhism, Jainism, Arya Samaj, Brahmo Samaj, Mahayana Buddhism, and Ravada Buddhism.

In the 1600s, the American colonies had a reputation as a safe place to go for the religious radicals. The area of land in America that became the central place to go was a section between Albany and Buffalo, New York. It was known as the "Burned-over District" and became the birthplace of Seventh Day Adventism, Jehovah's Witnesses, Millerism, Universal Friends, Oneida Society, Mormonism, Spiritualism, Koreshanity, and the American Shakers.

Eventually, these kinds of religious groups spread up into New York City, including Pentecostalism, Christian Science, the international peace movement, and Father Divine, who thought he was God living on Earth. He was one of the first of the leaders to have a cause of human rights.

During the 1960s, things were very turbulent in the United States. Violence within the human rights movement was becoming the norm, the Cold War with Russia was building, President Kennedy and other prominent figures were assassinated, the Vietnam War was ongoing, and the general population no longer trusted their government. The counterculture was starting to look for something new. Something built more on peace and love instead of money and war. So, these charismatic prophet-like figures from around the world began to take rise in the nation. They were seemingly the ones with the answers to solve the problems of the day.

Not all leaders of religious movements have evil intent. Quite a few of them start out believing what they are saying in their sermons and doing in their lives. But when those leaders take their social justice appeals to attract followers, and then later use those appeals to manipulate people, that is when the movement becomes a cult.

There are nine key characteristics of people vulnerable to cults. Keep in mind, though, that just because someone has one, or any of these traits, it does not mean they'll want to join a cult or fall victim to one. It is, however, important to know how cults operate and the types of mind games they might play so that they'll seem like less of a cure-all. We all want to belong, and we all want to have our 'group.' Despite what cults say, there are far better ways to go about this. People who might be susceptible to cults include

- **Those who need to feel validated** – Most everyone is seeking approval to some degree. We all want our friends to like us, to feel accepted at work, and so on. This desire is perfectly natural. However, those who need validation to function in society may be at risk of falling prey to cults.
- **Those who are seeking an identity** - Folks who are desperately searching for approval may be more likely to join a cult, as a way of feeling like they belong. And the same is true for people who are searching for their identity. That's not to say that people who are looking for new friends or those who feel lonely are going to get swept up in a cult. But it is true many cults prey on this desire.
- **Those who are followers and not leaders** – Cults are often centered around a strong leader. Typically, they are dynamic, warm, and inspiring — all traits that can be incredibly attractive to someone whose personality lends itself to following others, instead of being a leader themselves.
- **Those who are seeking meaning** - We all want to figure out the meaning of life, find our

purpose, and learn more about ourselves. But people who are desperate seekers of truth may be more likely to get caught up in a group that offers quick answers to their questions or promises a future that seems more meaningful and brighter.

- **Those who have schizotypal thinking** - Schizotypal thinkers walk along the edge of schizophrenia, without actually having the delusions or disconnection from society associated with the disorder. They have odd beliefs and behaviors that might fall into the realm of conspiracy-type, alien-type, or supernatural-type beliefs. Most cults propagate these strange ideas, doctrines, and beliefs.
- **Those who are highly suggestible** - Cults work by brainwashing their members, and anyone can fall victim to their mind games. But this is even more likely for someone who tends to be highly suggestible or gullible, especially if that person wants to find meaning in life so desperately that they are willing to give anything a go. This way of thinking is why it becomes difficult for a cult member to leave the group, once they've gone down the proverbial rabbit hole. You gamble with every step you take and faith you invest in a cult; you're simply hoping for the desired outcome of your investment. Often, you feel you've invested so much that it would be impossible to leave because that guarantees you've lost everything.
- **Those who always blame others** - People

who take no personal responsibility for their actions, and who would instead defer to a higher power to account for their behavior, may also be more likely to join a cult. Blamers make perfect cult members, as they are great at following others and have no moral issues with doing so, regardless of the consequences.

- **Those who are always angry** - If someone is angry or disgruntled, they are potentially more susceptible to cults or other extremist groups. Extremist groups/cults will provide them with a sense of belonging, a sense of 'us versus them,' a sense of blaming the 'other,' and being more 'right' or 'true.' Humans are, by nature, social animals with a strong need to belong, and when someone doesn't have that sense of belonging in their life, they can find it in cults and extremist groups. That's not to say that anyone who feels angry will up and join a cult. But if a cult comes along and plays into that anger in just the right way, they may be more likely to be a victim.
- **Those who have very low self-worth** - Cults prey on folks who feel like outsiders, so it's easy to see why low self-esteem may make someone more likely to get swept up in a group that tricks them and tries to make them feel like they belong. The cult can either confirm their low sense of selfworth and offer them a path to 'salvation,' or it can falsely raise their sense of self-worth by making them part of a chosen

group. It's a ploy to get new people to join, and it often works.

TODAY'S THREAT

Our world of constant communication with more people at one time than we have ever had before creates an even more significant threat of succumbing to the trappings of cults and conspiracies. This 24-hour, seven day a week connection to social media creates social isolation, which is now being recognized in countries around the world as a public health threat.

As fewer people take part in the old standards of the community, such as churches, night clubs, and families sitting down for dinner together, people are becoming further withdrawn that ends up in a void.

The virtual world has filled that void among the youngest of our society. We are no longer geographically bound to each other. We now search out online communities that have similar beliefs as we do and make connections as smoothly and powerfully as we used to years ago after meeting people in person and interacting with them.

Today's online world gives a platform for a new type of leader or prophet of a movement that we probably wouldn't have been exposed to so easily years ago. When you are in these groups, listening to the speaker explain their religion to you, you are alone, except for others in the same group helping to reinforce the movement. That isolation gives people who believe themselves to be alienated from mainstream culture an alternative reality to live within.

Whether the alternative reality is online or inperson at

a cult meeting, it builds on the promise of social justice, or the promise of a better, happier life. They all use the same method of control, which is extremely hard to escape.

DOOMSDAY CULTS

The term "Doomsday Cults" refers to cults that believe in apocalypticism - the religious belief that there will be an apocalypse. Initially, the word "apocalypse" referred to a revelation, but now it usually refers to the idea that the end of the world is imminent, even within one's lifetime.

This belief is usually accompanied by the idea that civilization will soon come to a tumultuous end due to a catastrophic global event. These views and movements often focus on cryptic revelations about a sudden, dramatic, and cataclysmic intervention of God in history; the judgment of all men; the salvation of the faithful elect; and the final rule of the elect with God in a renewed heaven and earth.

Arising initially in Zoroastrianism, one of the world's oldest continuously practicing religions, apocalypticism, or "the end of humanity," was developed more fully in later religions such as Judaism, Christianity, and Islam. However, these beliefs in radical changes to society after a major transformative event are not only religion-based. Millenarianist movements, groups that believe there will be radical transformations on particular thousand-year periods, can be secular, not espousing a specific religion. They can be social or political in nature.

The hardest thing to explain about the followers of these doomsday groups is the commitment of members to their cult. They remain committed even after the prophecies of the leader have turned out false. It has been called "Dissonance Reduction," which is a form of rationalization and a coping mechanism. Members of the cult seem to get a renewed vigor of the cult's cause after the failed prophecy, with explanations such as they did things that forestalled the disaster in effect, they saved the world.

Some researchers believe that the use of the term "doomsday cults" by the government and the news media can lead to a self-fulfilling prophecy, in which actions by authorities reinforce the apocalyptic beliefs of the group, which in turn can inspire further controversial actions. Group leaders object to being compared with other groups and parallels being drawn between the concept of a self-fulfilling prophecy and the theory of a deviancy amplification spiral.

The actual term "Doomsday Cult" was first used in the title of a 1966 scholarly study of a group of Unification Church members by John Lofland. It seemed that people turned to a cataclysmic world view after they had repeatedly failed to find meaning in any mainstream movements.

Social scientists have found that while some group members left after the date of a doomsday prediction by the leader passed uneventfully, others felt their belief and commitment to the group strengthened. Often when a group's doomsday prophecies or predictions fail to come true, the group leader will simply set a new date for impending doom or predict a different type of catastrophe on a different date. Niederhoffer and Kenner stated,

---

"When you have gone far out on a limb, and so

> many people have followed you, and there is much 'sunk cost,' as economists would say, it is difficult to admit you have been wrong."

In *Experiments With People: Revelations from Social Psychology*, Abelson, Frey, and Gregg explained further,

---

> "...continuing to proselytize on behalf of a doomsday cult whose prophecies have been disconfirmed, although it makes little logical sense, makes plenty of psychological sense if people have already spent months proselytizing on the cult's behalf. Persevering allows them to avoid the embarrassment of how wrong they were in the first place."

The common-held belief in a catastrophic event occurring on a future date can have the effect of ingraining followers with a sense of uniqueness and purpose.

After a failed prophecy, a member will attempt to explain the outcome through rationalization.

Explanations may include stating that the group members had misinterpreted the leader's original plan, that the cataclysmic event itself had been postponed to a later date by the leader, or that the activities of the group itself had forestalled disaster. In the case of the Festinger study, when the prophecy of a cataclysmic flood was proven false, the members pronounced their faith in God had prevented the event. They then proceeded to attempt to convert new members with renewed strength.

In his book, *Politeia: Visions of the Just Society*, Eric Carlton debates whether or not the term "doomsday cults" is appropriate to describe these types of groups. Carlton writes that the event is only seen as a "doomsday" for the "wicked and unrepentant," whereas members of the group itself often regard it as a "day of deliverance," or a "renewal of the world." He considers these groups as "the ultimate in exclusivity," and while the future will be bleak for nonbelievers due to an unforeseen cataclysm, members of the group are promised existence in a new utopia.

II

CULTS IN ACTION

"A long time ago being crazy meant something. Nowadays everybody's crazy." - Charles Manson

2

JIM JONES

"To me Death is not a fearful thing; it's living that is a curse." - Jim Jones

---

PEOPLES
TEMPLE
OF THE
DISCIPLES OF CHRIST

ONCE UPON A TIME...

It was 1978. I had just turned 16-years-old and was very excited. Not about finally being able to get my driver's license like so many of my classmates. I was born autistic, and just mastered the ability to ride a ten-speed bicycle. My 'coming-of-age' excitement was all about gaining the freedom to make my own choices, like whether to grow my hair long, wear flare pants or platform shoes, and whether to go out to the then-popular discos or not.

Amid all this teenage excitement, I also heard news stories about hundreds of people that had committed suicide somewhere down in South America. The name "Jim Jones" was repeated over and over, but I had no idea who he was or what the "People's Temple" was.

AND SO IT BEGAN...

Jim Jones was the leader of the People's Temple of the Disciples of Christ, and subject of numerous movies, documentaries, and books since that dreadful day. On November 18, 1978, 912 members of the Temple committed suicide in Jonestown, Guyana. It was the largest cult death and remains the largest loss of civilian life for the United States until the September 11, 2001 terrorist attacks on the World Trade Center.

It all started in Indiana. James T. Jones married Lynetta Putnam in 1926 and they all moved into their new home in Indiana. They soon had a son, also named James, but they called him Jim. Shortly after his son's birth, James T., a World War 1 veteran, had a mental breakdown, leaving Lynetta to take over working full-time and looking after the finances of the family. Young Jim spent most of his days with his father, who spent his time drinking and smoking in pool halls while Lynetta worked at the Glass factory.

Jim Jones was first introduced to a church by Myrtle Kennedy. She was an evangelical neighbor that took care of Jim in the afternoons. He was fascinated with the Pentecostal Holy Rollers, who spoke in tongues and rolled around the floor to express their devotion to Christ.

Even in his youth, Jim Jones had a curiosity about death and propensity for preaching. He practiced giving sermons out in the woods alone. By the age of ten, he built an altar in the attic of his parent's house and invited his friends over. While dressed in a white sheet, he preached to them.

Friends of Jim Jones remembered him officiating funerals for dead animals. It was discovered later that he was killing those animals so he could have something to practice on.

One bizarre game that young Jim liked to play was to lead a group of his friends to a casket warehouse. After breaking in, they would all climb into a casket and pretend to be dead. He told them that this was a way to experience death. Oftentimes, they were spooked into not returning with Jones whenever he suggested playing the game again.

Jim Jones believed that God had given him the ability to fly. So when he tried jumping off the roof of the family home, it resulted in a broken arm. Jones worshipped Adolf Hitler and became interested in Communism. He joined the Christian Youth Fellowship, where Christian Communism was often the topic of conversation.

When Jones turned 18-years-old, his father died, and

he started working at Reid Memorial Hospital. There he met his future wife, Marceline Baldwin. They both worked in the morgue, preparing bodies to be picked up by the funeral director. Marceline was impressed by the way Jim worked with the dead bodies and loved the compassion he showed them.

About a year later, Jones decided to open a church in Indianapolis. Jones' message of integration among races caught on with the area's residents. This was around the time of Martin Luther King Jr. and the height of the civil rights movement. It was also around the time that the Klu Klux Klan was very active in Indianapolis. So, racial tensions were very high.

Jim and his wife, Marceline, created their ideal family by adopting six children from around the world, besides having a biological son. The Joneses were the first white family in the state to adopt a black child, James Warren Jones Jr. It caused a great deal of grief for Marceline, as every time she left her house, people would call her racist names and even spit at her. For some reason, the negative attention led Jones to start thinking the CIA was watching him and tapping his phone lines. He also started to think his food was being poisoned.

In 1961, the United States was in a cold war with the Soviet Union, and Jones claimed that Indianapolis was going to be the target of a nuclear bomb. He sought out the safest place to live. An article in Esquire magazine claimed Eureka, California, a coastal city about 270 miles north of San Francisco, was the best place to live. Convinced, he decided to move the People's Temple west, to the Redwood Valley, near Ukiah, California.

In their new home among his followers, Jones started

dramatically casting cancer out of his audience members using the entrails of chickens. His popularity rapidly grew when word got out about his ability to help the sick become well again. People such as Elmer & Deanna Mertle, quit their jobs, sold their home and moved to Ukiah so they could be close to Jones. Deanna believed that Jones cured their 17-year-old son of a heart condition, telepathically.

The loving behavior of Jones, who was helpful to seniors, delicate with children, and supportive with the sick, wouldn't last long. After the Mertles moved and were able to attend Jones' sermons live, they noticed there was a disciplinary regime they never knew of before. Jones beat the couple's 16-year-old daughter with a paddle, on stage in front of six hundred people in the audience. She was accused of being a lesbian after she was seen kissing another female. By the end of the beating, the child's bottom looked like ground hamburger meat, and she couldn't sit for over a week.

Despite this embarrassing discipline of their daughter, the Mertles stayed with the People's Temple. By this time, they no longer had any money of their own, a home, or jobs. As with many cults like the People's Temple, followers gave the church all of their money and possessions, quit their work, and moved into some sort of compound or ranch-style property to live. Their new jobs became working for the church, doing things such as yard work, housework, promoting, and soliciting new members.

The Mertles finally left the church in 1974 and became vocal opponents of Jones. They eventually opened the Human Freedom Center to help cult defectors and People's

Temple survivors. In February 1980, the Mertles, including their daughter, were found murdered in their home.

Nobody has ever been arrested for the killings.

Around this time, Jones started to have bodyguards with him at all times. It might have been because of the thousands of dollars the church was bringing in daily, some days up to $25,000, or it might have been because Jones was becoming noticeably more paranoid since the acceleration of his drug use.

The People's Temple started gaining attention from very high-profile people, such as the Mayor of San Francisco, President Carter's wife, Rosalyn, Jane Fonda, and more. With this attention came tremendous political power, with its sheer number of followers. The People's Temple could influence local elections as it was estimated he controlled about 16% of the voters during off-year elections.

Jones' followers have been credited with helping elect progressive leaders, most notably San Francisco Mayor George Moscone and City Supervisor Harvey Milk, from not only having his followers' canvas for them but voting for them as well. Jones even organized mass voting fraud by sending his followers by the busloads to different areas of California to vote for the candidate that he wanted to win. Jones was rewarded for his efforts with a position on the San Francisco Housing Authority in 1976, which soon led to him being the chairman of the board. The People's Temple hosted fancy dinners with several of California's political delegates, even Governor Jerry Brown.

Behind the scenes of Jones' positive and supporting image, he was holding what became known as 'suicide drills.' Witnesses later testified about evening meetings where Jones had paper cups filled with wine passed out to them after telling them they were celebrating. After a few toasts and everyone had imbibed on their cup of wine, Jones told them they had just drunk poison, and within 30 minutes, they would all be dead. Some of the group panicked and started to cry, but most of them just sat in the venue, silent and contemplating their lives. After 45 minutes passed, Jones told them that this had only been a drill, and none of them were going to die. He just wanted to test their loyalties. It was just a test that they passed.

In the summer of 1977, ten former members of the group went on record in an article called "Inside People's Temple" in *New West Magazine*. In the article, they shared their firsthand experiences of living at the People's Temple under Jones' control. They revealed his all-night meetings and how they caused them mental anguish. They talked about the physical abuse, public beatings, and fake healings performed by Jones. A lot of influential people were defending Jones, such as California Lieutenant Governor Mervyn Dymally, who sent *New West Magazine* a message telling them to leave Jones alone. New West claimed to have received over 50 phone calls and 70 letters per day during the weeks leading up to them publishing the article, demanding that they not publish it.

On August 1, 1977, Jones left America and traveled to Guyana, just a few hours before the New West article about him and his followers hit the newsstands. Guyana was where Jones established and built Jonestown. Soon after, his followers in America packed up what belongings they could and followed him. Many of them left without telling any of their friends and families where they were going.

The Temple followers were excited about going to the new promised land called Jonestown. It was going to be a paradise, virtually heaven on earth. Oddly, upon their arrival, they were forced to surrender their passports, money, jewelry, and all other valuables to the Jonestown officials.

Jonestown sat on 3,800 acres of land that Jones had leased from the Guyanese government. Guyana was the only English-speaking socialist country located in South America. His lease was for 25 years, and he paid only 25 cents per acre of land. Jones' ties were so close to the higher-ups in the Guyanese government that he was able to have his boats come and go without inspection by Guyanese customs.

The land that Jones leased was rugged terrain, and he used 1,000 of his followers to cut the wood, build the houses, weed, and garden to get his community up and running. Former members of Jonestown remember those times as fun, exciting and they loved doing the work. It was an opportunity for the impoverished African Americans among his followers to be an equal part of a community finally.

His followers seemed lost in the dream that Jones had created for them, not realizing that they were living an isolated and controlled life. Every day they were up by 6 a.m. to eat a breakfast of rice, watery milk, and brown sugar, and sent to work until dark in 100-degree temperatures. Their lunch break would also consist of rice, and when they finally returned at the end of the day, they would get more rice and a shower.

After their dinner, there was a Russian language class, as Jones wanted his followers to be ready for their move to the Soviet Union one day. Jones wanted his Temple to be located as far away from America as possible and considered the Soviet Union to be the ultimate country to live in because of their communist lifestyle.

Jones' paranoia was accelerating even further, and it started to wear on his followers. He continued his public humiliations, beratings, and beatings of followers during his sermons. He preached that none of them could ever go back to America, as they were trying to get rid of the blacks and Native Americans.

He convinced them that the only place for them was in Jonestown. However, several followers were expressing interest in leaving, not only because of the hard-living but because they were homesick. There was a reward given to Temple members if they informed on others who talked about leaving. Jones sent those members who wanted to leave to his 'Extra Care Unit' where they were drugged for as long as it took for them to lose their ability to think coherently. Armed guards were posted around the compound and from a watchtower to make sure nobody could escape.

Jones started using even more drugs. He began slurring his words during his sermons, and often stumbled or tripped. He was frequently sick and claimed somebody was trying to poison him. Once, he even claimed someone shot him in the woods. The drugs Jones was taking and the amount wasn't uncovered until after the massacre, when several needles, morphine, hundreds of valium pills, and other barbiturates were discovered.

The Temple was facing many legal battles. Family members filed lawsuits as parents were trying to get their children back to America. Previous temple members who had fled Guyana were also suing. As a result of these legal issues, Jones started to initiate what he called 'white nights,' where temple members were awakened by loud sirens at 3 a.m. and told to assemble in the main pavilion. Inside they were instructed to drink what they were told was poison. Within a few hours of his followers drinking the poison, Jones came over the loudspeaker to announce that this was only a test to see who was still loyal to him. Jones also claimed the compound was surrounded by enemies who wanted to capture and torture them if they tried to leave.

Congressman Leo Ryan, who represented the San Mateo County, became very concerned when he heard of the lawsuits against Jones and the rumors that his followers were all being held in Jonestown against their will. Ryan mobilized a delegation, including reporters, and went to Jonestown to see for himself what was going on down there.

Ryan's group arrived on November 17, 1978, without any protection from the State Department. They had no reason to think there would be any violence. They were given a grand tour of the compound, which included a medical clinic, daycare, store, and plenty of homes for the members. They seemed impressed by how far the community had come and how happy the members seemed.

That evening after the tour, there was a grand show held at the main pavilion. Singers, dancers, and entertainers performed several shows. Afterward, Ryan made an announcement telling the crowd he believed Jonestown was the best thing that could have happened to them.

The next day the journalists conducted several interviews among the members and even Jim Jones himself.

Jones appeared to be drugged and worried about being shot by the reporters. At some point during the interviews, a note was passed to one of the reporters asking for help to get some of the temple members out of Jonestown. Jones responded to the journalists by telling them that anyone is free to leave if they wanted.

After this declaration, several of Jones' followers stepped forward to leave the compound. Disturbed by their choice to leave, temple member Don Sly, pulled a knife on Congressman Ryan and stabbed him. Ryan and his team decided to leave right then, instead of receiving medical care and staying the night. He gathered his team, the reporters, and the members that wanted to leave Jonestown and headed toward the airstrip at Port Kaituma, about 6 miles from Jonestown, where the plane was parked.

Ryan's group was loading their luggage, and some of the temple members on the plane when a tractor full of People's Temple guards carrying rifles drove up behind them. Even though Ryan and the others tried to find shelter, hiding behind the tires of the plane, or anywhere they could find, the guards started shooting everyone they could. Congressman Ryan was shot more than 20 times and died at the scene, along with some of the reporters and crew members. Ten of the Ryan team were either killed or laid motionless, pretending to be dead. They were left for 22 hours before they were rescued.

MASSACRE

During the Ryan attack, back in Jonestown, Jones' wife Marceline, ordered the temple members to go back to their cabins to calm down and get some rest. Within an hour,

Jones came over the loudspeaker telling everyone to go to the pavilion immediately. After everyone was assembled, Jones said he had a premonition the Congressman's plane would be shot down, and the Guyanese Defense Force was heading to Jonestown to shoot everyone there.

Jones went on to tell his followers that the Americans would soon follow, and everything would be ruined. The only thing they could do now was to die with respect. He asked if anyone disagreed with his plan. One of his followers asked if they could go to Russia, and he told her that he was trying to get Russia on the phone. The woman continued to shout out to Jones, only to be silenced by the crowd.

Jones ordered the Jonestown doctor to start administering the medication.

A few members carried a large stainless-steel tub into the pavilion. It was filled with a milky-white Flavor Aid (a cheaper store-brand of Kool-Aid) laced with cyanide. The babies and children were given the poison first, by using a plastic syringe and squirting it down the child's throat. The famous recording that Jones made during the mass suicide is often played on the news. Jones can be heard saying, "Mother, mother, mother, mother, please," in an attempt to stop the mothers from resisting the murder of their children.

The adults were given a full cup or glass of the poisoned flavor-aid, and if they didn't take it, they were held down and forced to drink it. Guards walked the members out of the pavilion after they drank their poison, and they were told to lay down on the ground. This was done to make room for those who still needed to be poisoned. Jones knew it was only a matter of time before the authorities arrived, and he didn't want any survivors left.

Throughout this whole process, Jones continued to encourage his followers to kill themselves, assuring them that death was only stepping over into another realm and that all good communists die with dignity, not hysterics.

The massacre was run like an assembly line – people entered the pavilion, drank their poison, exited the pavilion to the outside area, and laid down on the ground to die. The members waiting in line to get their dose of poison couldn't help but see the effects the poison had on the others: convulsions, cries of pain, vomiting, and loud gasps for air, all within five minutes of receiving their poison.

Eventually, all of the 900 plus members, including 300 children, died in the muddy land known as Jonestown.

Jones himself did not submit to such a gory death. Instead, his body was found on the ground where he sat issuing orders to his followers. He died of a gunshot to the head.

AFTERMATH

It was days until the authorities arrived at Jonestown. By then, most of the bodies had already started to decompose, lying throughout the grounds, bloated and oozing. In some cases, the rescuers had to scrape the remains into body bags. The Temple Guards were also ordered to shoot all of the animals that lived in Jonestown, including cats, dogs, and their chimpanzee named Mr. Muggs.

There were only a few survivors of the Jonestown massacre, a group of 11 members hiked about 30 miles through the jungle to escape. One of the survivors, Leslie Wagner-Wilson, made the trip with her three-year-old son on her back. I interviewed her for my radio show after she wrote a book about her life. Wagner-Wilson returned to America only to live a broken life on the streets, addicted to drugs. She eventually recovered later in life, but the shattering memories are still alive in her mind.

Odell Rhodes, another survivor, took the opportunity to disappear when the Jonestown doctor, Dr. Schacht, sent him to get her a stethoscope. There were a few others that hid under their bed and even under the bodies of other dead members.

Some members were away from Jonestown performing duties for Jones at the time of the massacre. One of those was Jim Jones Jr., who was at a basketball tournament in Georgetown, Guyana. He was eventually made aware of the killings from a call over the radio.

Jones also instructed three of his top members to take half a million dollars in cash to the Soviet Embassy in Georgetown, just before the massacre started that day.

It was another few days after the massacre when America sent hundreds of troops down to Jonestown. They brought helicopters so they could fly over the jungle to look for possible survivors. They only found 12 people and soon realized that most of the members of the People's Temple died the day of the massacre.

Eventually, when the authorities started to remove the bodies, they discovered there were layers of more uncounted dead bodies below them, invisible to the troops and media flying overhead. Air Force Captain John J. Moscatelli reported to *The Washington Post*,

> "Under adults, we found smaller adults and children, and under them more small babies."

Emergency responders spent eight days collecting the bodies into plastic bags to get a count. Nine of the bodies, including Congressman Ryan, had an autopsy performed in Georgetown. The rest of the bodies were packed into aluminum coffins and transported back to Dover Air Force Base in Delaware on cargo planes. All but 248 of the dead were identified and released to their family members. The unidentified 248 were buried in a mass grave at Evergreen Cemetery in Oakland, California.

The few survivors back in Guyana were taken to the Park Hotel to face several reporters from around the world, who inundated them with questions. Hundreds of reporters wanted to know the story and they were relentless. It was about a month before the survivors were able to fly back to the states. On arrival, they all had their passports seized from federal agents and made to pay a registration fee.

Journalists were cleared to travel to Jonestown, and Charles Krause of The Washington Post reported,

---

> "Jonestown from the sky literally looked like a garbage dump where somebody dumped a lot of rag dolls. The smell of death was so overpowering that it could be smelled inside the airplane 300 flying feet above."

Reporters were also allowed to go into Jones' house and reported finding several books and magazines about communism and conspiracies, along with a stockpile of drugs. Also found in the house were Jones' letters addressed to his father, which provided insight about himself.

Jones' wife, Marceline, also died in Jonestown, and her parents back in Indiana received both her and Jim's body to have a funeral. When the Doan & Mills Funeral Home, located in Richmond, Indiana, set up the funerals, several of the members from the People's Temple in California planned to attend. But when the FBI heard about this, they wanted a layout of the building for security purposes. Information about the funeral soon made the media outlets and protests began. Soon the funeral was cancelled due to threats of attacks on the funeral home. Marceline was eventually buried at the Indiana Earlham Cemetery without announcements or problems. Jim Jones was cremated; his ashes were thrown in the ocean.

At first, the deaths at Jonestown were considered a mass suicide, but as police investigated further, the people that died there became murder victims.

There was only one member of the People's Temple arrested and charged with crimes relating to Jonestown, Larry Layton. Layton was the man responsible for the shooting of Congressman Ryan and Richard C. Dwyer, the Deputy Chief of the U.S. Mission in Guyana, who had also been shot at the airstrip with Ryan, but he survived.

Layton first stood trial in November of 1978, on four charges – conspiring in the murder of Congressman Leo Ryan, aiding and abetting in the murder of Leo Ryan, conspiracy in the attempted murder of Richard Dwyer, and aiding and abetting in the attempted murder of Richard Dwyer. But the trial ended in a hung jury.

It was another nine years before Layton was finally convicted on all four charges in March 1987. During the nine years Layton waited for his litigation to be final, he was released on bail, worked and was able to lead a regular life as a free man in the community. Layton had to work under an assumed name to protect his identity, as well as any of his family members that lived with him. Finally, in March of 1987, the second and final trial would commence. But this time, Layton was convicted on all charges and sentenced to the mandatory life required by the Court.

The remaining People's Temple members appealed to then, President Bill Clinton, for a pardon, which never materialized. Layton was eventually granted an early release and left prison in 2002 after serving fifteen years in prison. He now lives in Northern California.

When Congressman Ryan went to Guyana, he brought with him an aide by the name of Jackie Speier, who, during the attack on Ryan's group at the airstrip, took cover under one of the wheels of the plane. But one of the attackers came up behind her and shot her too. Even though Speier played dead on the ground after being shot, the attacker decided to shoot her a few more times to make sure that she was dead. Only, Speier was still alive. She was found, brought back to America, and amazingly recovered. In 2008, Speier won Ryan's old seat on Congress, and at the time of writing this book, she still holds it.

SO NOW WHAT?

Jim Jones Jr. spent the first 15 years after the massacre going by the name "James Jones." He appeared on several popular television talk-shows of the time, such as Oprah Winfrey. The following is an excerpt from some of their conversation during one of her shows in October 2010.

He told Oprah that he forgives his father, who had a mental illness, drug abuse, and unchecked power.

> "Nine hundred people died, and I miss them every day. But I also recognize that they tried. They tried something—they failed horrifically —but they tried, and out of that, I've taken a lot of pride to realize that I'm Jim Jones Jr. I can't hide from that."

The Guyanese government always considered the Jonestown Massacre an American problem, so they never investigated it. It took until 2009 for the Guyana government to finally erect a plaque commemorating the victims. Their government has just recently started to arrange tours to the site. There is an overwhelming feeling that Guyana wants to move forward for the lives of their people, and not mention the massacre unless they have to.

Nobody has ever tried to settle or rebuild the old Jonestown compound, mainly because of a great fear of Jonestown being haunted by evil spirits. According to Caribbean lore, the spirits of dead people, typically evil ones, are called jumbies.

Over the last decades, none of the hundreds of buildings are left, and there are only a few of the support poles from the pavilion remaining. What abandoned equipment has all rusted to an unusable state. The main grounds of the compound, where nearly a thousand bodies laid dead for days before they were retrieved, have all been covered in overgrown weeds and out of control bushes.

At the end of 1978, the Temple declared bankruptcy, and its assets went into receivership. In light of lawsuits, on December 4, 1978, Charles Garry, the corporation's attorney, petitioned to dissolve the People's Temple. The petition was granted in San Francisco Superior Court in January 1979. A few Temple members remained in Guyana through May 1979 to wrap up the movement's affairs, then returned to the U.S.

The Temple's buildings in Los Angeles, Indianapolis, and Redwood Valley are intact, and some are used by church congregations. The Central Spanish Seventh-day Adventist Church is at the Temple's former Los Angeles building at 1366 South Alvarado Street. The Temple's former San Francisco headquarters (1859 Geary Blvd.) was destroyed in the 1989 Loma Prieta earthquake; a Post Office branch now occupies the site.

A FINAL THOUGHT ABOUT THE PEOPLE'S TEMPLE

Here is an excerpt from a recent interview by Caitlin Gibson of *The Washington Post* on November 18, 2018 of Charles Krause, a Washington Post foreign correspondent at the time.

Krause had come to South America along with California Congressman Leo J. Ryan and his entourage to visit a remote cult compound known as Jonestown. Forty years ago, Charles Krause lay on the tarmac of a remote jungle airstrip in Guyana, shot in the hip, holding still and pretending to be dead:

> "Forty years later, in a world that has changed in so many ways, do you think this sort of thing could happen again?
>
> Yes, there is the potential for it to happen again. It has happened again a number of times. We've had Waco, and we've had other incidents where it's not as many people, but it's the same sort of situation. I feel strongly that we need to be more skeptical about political or religious leaders who promise things, who seem to be hypocritical, who talk the talk but don't walk the walk."

3

AUM SHINRIKYO SUPREME TRUTH

"I would go to interminable hell if I kill the guru. I cannot betray the guru." - former senior Aum Shinrikyo member Yoshihiro Inoue

---

There are approximately 9 million passengers that ride Tokyo's subway every day. On the morning of March 20, 1995, five members of the Aum Shinrikyo cult boarded different trains at the ends of three separate lines

that connect at the Kasumigaseki, Japan's government building.

The height of Tokyo's rush hour was between 8 a.m. and 9 a.m. on Mondays to Fridays. It was approximately 8:15 a.m. when each of the cult members boarded their respective trains with an umbrella and a duffle bag full of the deadly nerve gas, sarin.

Just before they were scheduled to arrive at the next station, each cult member poked a hole in their duffle bag with the point of their umbrella. Then each member exited the train, leaving the duffle bags to leak out the sarin gas.

The leader of the Aum Shinrikyo, Shoko Asahara, planned to take over the world by first paralyzing the Japanese government with this attack. In the end, the cult killed 12 innocent people and injured 5,000 more in this massacre.

THE BEGINNING

The cult, Aum Shinrikyo, whose name means "supreme truth," had over 2,000 members worldwide. Aum Shinrikyo, often shortened to Aum, started in 1984 in Shoko Asahara's one-bedroom apartment located in the commercial business district of Tokyo. In the first few years, he mainly gave yoga and meditation classes, but by 1989, it was officially recognized as a religious organization. Asahara claimed he wanted to restore original Buddhism, and his beliefs drew on aspects of Indian Buddhism, Tibetan Buddhism, and Hinduism. The group attracted a large number of graduates from Japan's elite universities and was later dubbed a "religion for the elite."

Shoko Asahara was born Chizuo Matsumoto. He only

had partial sight in his right eye, so he was educated at a school for the blind. Shinrikyo was married in 1978, and with money from his parents, set up an acupuncture clinic, where he sold fake medicine to patients. Eventually, he was prosecuted for fraud for selling a rheumatism medicine proven to be fake.

Shinrikyo once took a trip to the Himalayas, where he claimed to have levitated. He even produced a photograph of him appearing to float in mid-air. Asahara declared himself to be Christ and claimed he was chosen to lead God's army during the coming Armageddon at the end of the century.

Asahara outlined his doomsday prophecy, that included a third world war initiated by the United States, which he described as a nuclear Armageddon.

The war would bring an end to humanity, except for those that joined the group. The Aum cult's mission was not only to spread the word of salvation but to survive end times. The date for the Armageddon was predicted to occur in 1997. Asahara claimed the United States would start the end of the world by attacking Japan. Asahara saw dark conspiracies everywhere he looked, promulgated by Jews, Freemasons, The Dutch, British Royal family, and Japanese religions.

CREATE THE ENEMY

In 1989, an anti-cult lawyer, Tsutsumi Sakamoto, started a class-action lawsuit against the Aum Shinrikyo cult. Sakamoto had successfully led a class-action lawsuit against the Unification Church, also known as the Moonies, on behalf of the relatives of Unification members. Several members of Aum complained of being held against their will, having all of the money taken, and sexual abuse while being in the group.

In an interview with the *Tokyo Broadcasting System (TBS)*, Sakamoto described what the cult was doing to its members. He also had a vial of Shinrikyo's blood, that was tested for the 'Special Power' its leader claimed to have. Nothing unusual was found in the blood.

Before the TBS broadcasted the interview, they shared it with Aum members without telling Sakamoto and breaking the protection of their source.

Four days after Shinrikyo watched the interview on the TBS, Sakamoto, his wife, and son went missing from their apartment. The police believed that perpetrators broke into Sakamoto's house to commit a burglary and, somehow during the crime, decided to kidnap the family. In 1991, the police received a tip and reopened the murder case, but it would take another six years to learn the truth of what happened that night.

On November 3, 1989, several Aum members, including Hideo Murai, the cult's scientist; Sataro Hashimoto, a martial arts master; Tomomasa Nakagawa; and Kazuaki Okazaki drove to the train station where Sakamoto usually got off when he came home from work. But on this day, he didn't show up. The cult didn't know Sakamoto had stayed home from work that day for the Cultural Day holiday.

The group carried a duffle bag with 14 hypodermic syringes and potassium chloride, as they planned to kidnap Sakamoto from the train station. Changing the plan, the group then drove to Sakamoto's house and waited until 3 a.m. They entered the home through an unlocked door.

Sakamoto was attacked first, receiving a hit on the head with a hammer. Both his wife and son were beaten severely.

All three of the family were injected with the potassium chloride, and cloths placed over their faces. Sakamoto and his son died of toxic injection, but his wife did not. Instead, they strangled her to death. The group smashed each of their victim's teeth to make identification difficult. They placed each body into drums and buried them in separate jurisdictions a distance away from the Sakamoto house. In case one body was found, they wouldn't tie it to the missing family.

It wasn't until the Tokyo subway sarin gas attack that these members of Aum were arrested for the crimes against the Sakamoto family. Until then, police had no details of the Sakamoto family's fate. It would be another five years before the police would finally locate the missing bodies and convict the Aum members that were involved.

During the early 1990s, even though they were under investigation by the police, Aum continued its illegal activities. In July of 1993, cult members sprayed large amounts of a liquid containing Bacillus anthracis spores from the roof of their Tokyo headquarters with the hope of starting an anthrax epidemic. The attack only resulted in a large number of complaints about bad odors causing upset stomachs, but no infections. After their failed attempt at making anthrax, they decided they could produce sarin gas instead. In secret, they began manufacturing the deadly gas. They also manufactured VX gas – an extremely toxic synthetic nerve agent developed for military use in chemical warfare.

The cult first tested the sarin gas on sheep in a remote part of Western Australia, successfully killing about 30 sheep. Emboldened by their success, they attempted several assassinations, such as the people at Soka Gakkai (the Institute for Research in Human Happiness) and the cult satirical cartoonist Yoshinori Kobayashi. The cult now felt confident enough to take it to the next level.

On the evening of June 27, 1994, Aum decided to carry out a chemical weapons attack against civilians by releasing sarin gas in the Japanese city of Matsumoto. The cult members converted a refrigerator truck so that sarin would slowly be released in clouds as they drove around the city. The Aum had one neighborhood in particular in mind that housed several judges that were about to rule negatively on a real estate lawsuit that Aum had in court.

The Matsumoto Sarin attack resulted in 8 deaths and the wounding of over 500 others. The police initially blamed an innocent local resident Yoshiyuki Kouno, and never considered the Aum cult. It was only after the Tokyo subway sarin gas attack that Aum was discovered to be behind the Matsumoto sarin attack as well.

At 7 a.m. on December 12, 1994, two members of the Aum cult, followed a man on the streets of Osaka, who was considered a spy against the Aum group. As soon as they were close enough to him, they sprinkled a nerve agent comprised of VX gas. The victim was able to chase the cult members about 100 yards before he collapsed, fell into a coma, and died ten days later. He was the first person to die from the VX nerve agent. Two others were injured during this attack as well. Some of the nerve gas was thrown around during the scuffle between the cult members and the victim.

The last known significant crime credited to the Aum cult before the Tokyo subway was the kidnapping and murder of Kiyoshi Kariya, the brother of a cult member that escaped earlier that year. The cult believed by kidnapping Kariya, they could find the location of his sister. They took their captive to a compound near Mount Fuji, where they tortured him until he died. The body was destroyed in a microwave-powered incinerator, and the remnants were thrown into Lake Kawaguchi.

Finally, the day had come. Even though it was the day they had all prayed for and dedicated every action of their lives to, they were scared.

This day is what they had lived their lives for, to be one of the survivors chosen to move the world forward. The double chemical attack on the Tokyo subway on the morning of March 20, 1995, took the lives of 13 people, seriously injured 54, and hurt 980 others.

Over the next week, the full operation planned by Aum would be revealed for the first time. Police found explosives, chemical weapons, and a Russian Mil Mi-17 military helicopter at Aum's Mount Fuji compound. News in Japan claimed the Aum compound had biological warfare such as anthrax and Ebola, but that was later found not to be true. What the compound did have was sufficient chemicals to produce enough sarin to kill 4 million people.

Police also found other compounds with laboratories that manufactured drugs such as LSD, methamphetamine, and truth serum. The cult also possessed a safe, which contained millions of U.S. dollars in cash and gold. Some of these compounds had small jails that held prisoners of the cult.

It took six weeks to round up and arrest over 150 cult

members for a variety of offenses, but none of the leaders of the cult had been arrested. There wasn't enough evidence against them yet. During the arrests, the chief of the National Police Agency was shot four times near his home and seriously wounded. The cult was thought to be behind the shooting but was never charged.

During this time, several media outlets were camped in front of the Aum compound in Tokyo, trying to get pictures of any of the cult members. Hideo Murai, Aum's Minister of Science, was returning through the crowd of journalists, when he was stabbed to death in front of cameras by a member of Yamaguchi-gumi, one of the Korean organized crime syndicates. The killer was caught and convicted, but the motive behind the killing was never revealed.

In May, a burning paper bag was discovered in the bathroom at the Shinjuku train station. It was later revealed to be a hydrogen cyanide device. Had it not been extinguished in time, it would have released enough gas into the ventilation system to kill potentially 10,000 commuters.

On May 16, Asahara was finally found hidden in one of the compounds and arrested. The same day, the cult mailed a parcel bomb to the office of Yukio Aoshima, the governor of Tokyo, blowing the fingers off of his secretary's hand.

Asahara was charged with 23 counts of murder and 16 other offenses.

During his trial, Asahara often wore diapers and sat on a cushion. He stopped communicating with his children and his defense team. A court-appointed psychiatrist suggested he might be faking insanity to avoid punishment. Media outlets across Japan reported how Asahara had been deemed competent, but they failed to report on episodes of Asahara's behavior in his solitary confinement cell.

According the Nishiyama Report, during those episodes, Asahara:

> "...took off his trousers and diapers, exposed his genitalia, and masturbated. He repeated the same action frequently. Whenever he acts like that, he drops his trousers, his diaper and diaper cover to his knees, finishes the act, then raises his trousers up to his waist again."

Psychiatrists claimed in a report filed to the Tokyo High Court,

> "Death cult guru Shoko Asahara is merely trying to pull the wool over authorities' eyes to avoid the death sentence against him from being carried out."

The Nishiyama Report also stated,

> "In April 2005, just before the accused's lawyer entered a visiting room, the accused exposed his penis and began masturbating, continuing until he had finished while the lawyer stood before him the

> entire time. He has repeated this act of masturbation in the visiting room, as well as in his solitary confinement cell, since being placed under observation in May. He also performed the act in front of his daughters when they came to visit him in August of the same year."

Despite acknowledging acts such as the shameless masturbation in front of his adult daughters, the Nishiyama Report ruled

---

> "that Asahara had not lost his faculties to the extent that it should stop him from going into court."

However, Otohiko Kaga, a former Tokyo Detention Center psychiatrist and now novelist, slammed the Nishiyama Report after visiting Asahara a couple of days after the document had been publicly released.

> "As far as the false dementia goes, he understands language and can communicate verbally. False dementia really only should be used when there is absolutely no verbal communication evident. The thing I thought weirdest about the Nishiyama Report was that it didn't mention a single thing about what kind of person Asahara is, nor anything about his character. They knew without a doubt that

he was susceptible to going stir crazy. I really get the impression they were looking to get a result out quickly.

It's impossible for him to continue with his trial. One of my catatonic stupor patients always throws up whatever they eat. Sometimes, their vomit is unleashed so violently, it hits the ceiling. They unconsciously carry out acts that make others feel unpleasant. It's the same with Asahara brazenly masturbating in front of people, but it can be cured. They did it once at the Osaka Detention Center. They made all the death row prisoners take meals together and wiped out stir craziness pretty quickly. They need to change his circumstances, his environment, even just a little. I really think they should stop his trial temporarily and concentrate on his treatment."

The trial was called "the trial of the century" by the media, and Asahara was found guilty of the Tokyo subway attack and sentenced to death. Asahara also admitted that in January 1994, he ordered the murder of one of the other cult members, Kotaro Ochida, who worked as a pharmacist at an Aum hospital. Ochida tried to escape from the compound but was caught and strangled on the order of Asahara.

The senior members of the cult were also convicted and sentenced to death. Asahara appealed the conviction but was not successful. Asahara claimed he was not aware of the attacks that were carried out by the cult, because his health had deteriorated badly. Asahara decided to abandon his leadership role in the Aum.

In June, a copycat attack was launched by a hijacker on a Boeing 747 bound for Hakodate from Tokyo. He claimed to be a member of Aum, who possessed sarin gas and explosives. The authorities later found that not only did he not have any weapons, but he had also never been a member of Aum.

In July, several other cyanide devices were found at different locations throughout the Tokyo subway, but none of them were detonated, and nobody was injured.

On October 10, 1995, Aum was stripped of its official status as a legal, religious entity, and it declared bankruptcy in early 1996. The cult was allowed to operate under the constitutional guarantee of freedom of religion, but a successful computer business and donations now fund it. It is under rigorous surveillance. There have been several attempts to have the group banned, but none of them have succeeded.

The group has undergone several changes since the arrests and conviction of Asahara. Immediately after Asahara stepped down as leader, his two preteen sons officially replaced him as the guru and leaders. The group changed its name to "Aleph" in February of 2000. It announced a change of their doctrine and all religious texts related to the Vajrayana Buddhist doctrines and the Bible were removed. They also stopped the publication of their activities and beliefs.

The group apologized to the victims of the sarin gas attack and established a special compensation fund for them. By 1999, Fumihiro Joyu became the new leader for the Aum cult.

On July 6, 2018, Asahara and six other Aum Shinrikyo members (Yoshihiro Inoue, Tomomitsu Niimi, Tomomasa Nakagawa, Kiyohide Hayakawa, Seiichi Endo, and Masami Tsuchiya) were executed by hanging. Six more members were later executed by hanging on July 26, 2018. (Yasuo Hayashi, Kenichi Hirose, Toru Toyoda, Masato Yokoyama, Kazuaki Okazaki, and Satoru Hashimoto.)

On March 8, 2007, Fumihiro Joyu, formally announced a split in the group. Joyu's group would now be called 'Hikari no Wa (The Circle of Light) and claimed the new group was committed to uniting science and religion, thereby creating "the new science of the human mind." Joyu claimed he wanted to move the group away from its criminal history and toward a spiritual path.

The group now has about 1,500 members and has been actively trying to recruit new members through social media.

On New Year's Day in the Harajuku district of Tokyo, Kazuhiro Kusakabe intentionally rammed into pedestrians crowded on the narrow streets in retaliation for the execution of members of the Aum Shinrikyo. There was a total of nine people injured from the attack.

Both groups, 'Aleph' and 'Hikari no Wa,' have been formally designated as terrorist organizations by several countries, including the European Union, Canada, Kazakhstan, and the United States. Russia has gone even further by banning the group.

I interviewed a member of Aum. He didn't want his name to be published, so I have included parts of our communication:

> "When I was a child, I loved to play in sports and was a pretty good student. I was just really bored with what they were teaching me in school. I mean, what do they teach you in class that you will ever use in life? It really seemed like a memory class, just recite it back to the teachers, but not really know it.
>
> What I was looking for was some knowledge. I mean real knowledge, a kind of wisdom without waiting until you get old. They weren't teaching me that! They were just giving me superficial knowledge, nothing deep.
>
> It always seemed that people just went through the motions in life. Going day to day and never really growing or gaining anything that was useful, it was just all material things that you would buy with the money that you worked for. What kind of life is that?
>
> I don't think people really love each other; it's just something that they do. Real love doesn't include one person lying to another or hurting each other by abuse like it is. I think they get sexual and

romantic love mixed up with this real love, but that's not enough, it can never be enough.

I tried to learn different kinds of faith to try and get some answers, make things better. But it seemed that with every type of group I got involved with just didn't love me, or I didn't love them, I don't know. As time went by, I would spend far more time being depressed and not excited or happy about anything I did. It was all the same to me, and I started thinking about the ways in which I could end it.

I don't know why, but it was at this time that I started thinking about the afterlife. What was the afterlife? What does it mean to be dead? Could being dead really be any worse than it was to be alive, where I felt like a machine? These are the things that I would start to pursue, as I needed some answers, I needed to make my move, and start to feel something.

It seems that the world is filled with people that are suffering, hurting, and in a great deal of pain, and they didn't need to be. They look for their answers in addictions, like drugs, to take away the pain or deal with reality. Others eat too much just to cause themselves more pain. Everyone wants all of the things that they can't have or could ever have. This is what Aum did for me and others, take away all of that stress.

Aum Shinrikyo is a way to look at both the spiritual and physical worlds and give us the answers to both of them. You have to understand that science can only answer the questions of the physical world, not the emotional one. I mean, there are no ways that you could measure the spiritual world with scientific tools. They do not belong to the same world. It can only be measured by a spiritual being.

I first came across Aum Shinrikyo with a book about meditation. I started to attend classes at Aum and started to feel better about myself almost immediately. After a few months, I started to help out at the Aum temple by doing volunteer work. It was a matter of about a year before I started getting into the 'secret yoga' classes. That was when you were invited to do the class with a group leader of Aum. I could tell right away that my leader could see me, the real me, with no barriers. I was in my early twenties when I became a fulltime member and left my school and job. It was the late 1980s, and there were about 3,000 members back then.

My life in the Aum group was much harder than life out in the real world. But the big difference was that my soul felt good, and I didn't have any worries. It was all so carefree. I never had so much support or had so many friends before Aum either. The difference with my friends was that it felt like they were on the same journey as I was – to find my spiritual awakening.

There was a structure to my life that I never had before. It was so simple, just do as I am asked to do, and good things will happen. Now I know the media will call that mind control or brainwashing, but it's not. They don't try to report the facts, that doesn't get them ratings or sales. They need controversy, and it would be boring, just reporting that we were all very happy and really enjoying our lives.

We were all free to live our lives as we wanted, do what we wanted to do. There was no power control that had to give us permission to do what we wanted. I see people in the world that are like that, like in Russia or North Korea, and the world does nothing about them. The media told you that we couldn't go as we pleased, but that's not true. Yes, we didn't own anything like cars, but the temple had cars that we could use anytime that we wanted to."

When asked about the violent crimes committed by the group, such as the murder of the Sakamoto family:

"That kind of activity was kept secret from me, but no matter what was done by the leadership of Aum, it was done for the benefits, which would far outweigh anything that was bad for someone. I couldn't believe what was reported in the media as well, even though now that I think some of those things did occur. But I still don't think the group was capable of committing the Sakamoto murders as we were not a group that was organized that way. Plus, we were working like a communist group in the way that we worked as a group, so we knew what we were all doing.

I have felt nothing but gratitude and great fulfillment being part of the Aum. It seemed to be the higher I got in the group, the more at peace I was. The spiritual power was so strong that I needed a lot less sleep. We would take LSD for rituals called 'heat,' and you would have no sense of your body, only your mind. It was your subconscious becoming the real world. It would be part of the spiritual training to give yourself tough challenges of all kinds, and some of them included the drugs.

I first learned about the Tokyo subway sarin gas attack from a news flash on the internet. I didn't think Aum was involved at all, I didn't know who it did, but it certainly wasn't Aum. Our temple was raided by the police, so I left as they were only interested in the leadership. When Asahara was arrested, I didn't feel angry, as anger is a sign that you are spiritually immature. Inside the group, we went on as usual. Nothing changed as we continued our training.

When different members got arrested, and some of them confessed to the crime, as an Aum follower, it didn't matter if they had done it or not. All that was important was to continue our training. How we developed ourselves was far more important than whether Aum was guilty.

We wouldn't question the actions of our leaders as they had training at much higher levels than us. So even after the sarin gas attack, we didn't question our training or lifestyles. The Aum doctrine's high level called 'Vajrayana' was of great significance, but for us, it was like a star in the sky. It was too far away for us to possibly understand it. There were tens of thousands of years' worth of things that you had to accomplish before you could reach that level.

It is believed that if you were at such a high level, and had to kill someone, it would be in order to raise that person up. The person that you killed would be happier now than he was being alive. So, I understand that path. But again, that can only be done. If I would have been able to perceive what happens to a person after their death, and by killing them would raise them to a higher level, then maybe I would have been involved.

I am not saying that the Aum was correct in doing what they did, but there was value to it. I would like to use it to somehow benefit normal people. I am still in Aum because the benefits I've received are so great. It requires a kind of logical reversal. There are hopeful elements, and I'm trying to clearly distinguish what I understand from what I don't."

SARIN GAS

Sarin is a colorless, odorless, and liquid form synthetic compound that has been used as a chemical weapon because of its extreme toxicity as a nerve agent. Exposure is lethal even at very low concentrations. Death will usually occur within ten minutes after breathing the gas into the lungs, causing the lung muscle to be paralyzed, which results in asphyxia.

Initial symptoms following exposure are a runny nose,

tightness in the chest, and constriction of the pupils. Soon after that, nausea will occur, then drooling as control is lost of body functions. Vomiting, defecating or urinating, followed by twitching or jerking around is expected. Ultimately, the person becomes comatose and suffocates in a series of convulsive spasms.

Production and stockpiling of sarin was outlawed in April 1997 by the Chemical Weapons Convention of 1993. It was discovered in 1938 by German scientists at IG Farben, a German chemical and pharmaceutical conglomerate formed in 1925 from a merger of six chemical companies—BASF, Bayer, Hoechst, Agfa, Chemische Fabrik GriesheimElektron, and Chemische Fabrik vorm. Weiler Ter Meer. It was seized by the Allies after World War II and divided back into its constituent companies who were trying to create stronger, more efficient pesticides.

Sarin, tabun, and VX gases all have a very short shelf life. The CIA has reported the sarin gas that Iraq created only has a two-week shelf life. This short lifespan is the reason the cult kept two separate precursors that produce sarin when they are combined. They only produced the sarin immediately before they needed to use it.

Weaponizing nerve agents like sarin requires munitions that can disperse the gas in droplets, which will kill the intended victims on contact or vapor that is inhaled. Most explosive devices would either destroy the nerve agents upon detonation or fail to disperse them adequately.

Spraying of the nerve agents seemed to be the choice for most cults that used it, as it was usually the most effective and easiest way to do it. But as most experts say, pumping agents into a building's indoor ventilation system, even though it's not easy to do, is the most lethal method. Spraying outside has problems reaching the targets because there are so many variables that can't be controlled, such as weather, wind, temperature, sunlight, and rain.

When Aum first tried to spray sarin from a moving van, the sprayer malfunctioned and sprayed backward. In another attempt, Aum exposed their security chief to the nerve agent.

When Aum finally chose to carry out a gas attack on the subway by poking holes in the bags and leaving them on subway cars allowing the fumes to seep out, the result created chaos. Affected people littered the sidewalks and subway stations, foaming at the mouth, vomiting, and convulsing. The final analysis was about 85% of the 5,510 people treated at Tokyo's hospitals were there just because they were worried and not harmed. Twelve died from the sarin exposure, and about 40 were seriously injured, and slightly less than 1,000 were moderately sick.

4

ORDER OF THE SOLAR TEMPLE

"Our terrestrial journey is coming to an end" - The Last Voyage of the Solar Temple by Joseph DiMambro

The Solar Temple, founded by Luc Jouret in 1984, is also known as the Ordre du Temple Solaire (OTS).

It is a French Chivalric Organization of the Solar Tradition, relating to or connected with the system of chivalry that was believed in and followed by medieval knights and based on the ideas of the Knights Templar.

Luc Jouret was born in the Belgian Congo and belonged to the Belgian army in his younger years. He attended Brussels University and studied medicine, specializing in obstetrics. During the 1970s, he joined the Renewed Order of the Templars, which was a neo-Nazi organization led by the former Gestapo officer Julien Origas. Origas died in 1983, causing the Templars to break apart, and Jouret formed his group, calling it "Chivalric Order of the Solar Tradition" in Switzerland. This group mainly sold the idea of homeopathy and mysticism.

KEEPING UP WITH TRADITION

Within a year, the Chivalric Order merged with a cult called "The Foundation Golden Way," led by Joseph DiMambro, a homeopathic doctor, jeweller, and new age guru that drew upon metaphysical and mystic knowledge. The new group decided to change its name to "The Solar Temple," and Jouret was named the high priest. The members believed they were part of an unbroken lineage that dated back to the Knights Templar of the Middle Ages, the elite fighting squad that protected Christendom during the Crusades. The original order was thought to have been ended after charges of heresy. It was believed they were all burned at the stake in the early 1300s.

Similar to their medieval predecessors, the Solar Temple performed secret initiations, as well as rituals that involved prayers, swords, and champagne. Jouret gave the group sermons regularly that was not of the usual fare, with candles burning and everyone listening to a preacher and prayer. The room was fancily adorned, with music and sparkling champagne served. It was more like a cocktail party.

The Solar Temple cult was interested in attracting affluent 'yuppie' types that were young professionals and well-to-do. Their membership fees were high, so they did not target the transient uneducated person. Jouret recruited new members through a trendy homeopathic clinic he owned in Geneva. Outside of the cult, Jouret was a free-lance corporate motivator where he perfected his control techniques.

Perhaps the most famous member of the cult was Princess Grace of Monaco, previously known as actress Grace Kelly. The Sunday Times reported just after her death in 1982 that her initiation into the cult involved nude massage and ritualistic sex at a ceremony at the monastery in Ville-Morgon in France. Kelly was asked to donate 20 million Swiss francs to the Solar Temple, but she only ended up giving them 12 million. Shortly after her donation of the money, she started to feel some reservations about the group. She threatened to go to press with the truth about the Solar Temple. Two months later, while out driving with her daughter, their car drove over a mountainside and landed on a lawn owned by a Solar member. Kelly survived the crash but died the next day in the hospital.

In 1986, Jouret and DiMambro opened a branch of the cult in Canada, when they bought an old monastery in the north end of Montreal. Jouret toured Canada and gave lectures on management and motivation to large Canadian companies. He also traveled to smaller towns and gave seminars on homeopathy and growing organic foods. He even started to sell inspirational tapes to people through New Age shops.

It wasn't long before the cult started to attract prominent people living in Canada, such as the Mayor of Richelieu in Quebec. The membership fees in Canada were set at $50 a week, and they included access to lectures and seminars. If you wanted to move up in the group, you could buy a 'Club Arcadia' membership for $150 per week. This higher membership would allow you to work on the organic food farm that the cult opened.

For $200 a week, you would be included in the "Golden Circle," which allowed you to join in on the Temple's secret rituals. If you joined the highest tier, you were expected to turn all your savings and property over to the church.

Over the next couple of years, Jouret started to focus on an upcoming apocalypse rather than the homeopathic or holistic lifestyles. He told his members that there would only be 100 people elected to survive the impending doom and that he was the one to decide who those 100 would be. At this point, Jouret started to exert strict control over the cult members, such as telling them who they could marry and even dissolving existing marriages.

The change in the group's direction caused some members to become angry and leave. Claims from ex-cult members started to make the newspapers and provided details about what went on behind closed doors in the cult compounds. The people of Canada began speaking negatively about the cult, and its membership numbers started to decrease.

The 1980s brought a decline in the markets and property values, and Jouret and DiMambro had invested most of their money into properties. Between financial pressure and no new members joining the group, Jouret's sermons became very dark. He frequently discussed mass suicide.

In 1990, DiMambro's son, Eli, 29, became very outspoken about his father. He claimed that his father faked his rituals and mystical feats by using holograms, laser lights, and sound effects. The Solar Temple responded by saying that the magic tricks were stunts to keep the less-awakened members in the group. After this controversy, 15 members left the cult.

DiMambro had a 12-year-old daughter, Emmanuelle, who he forced to wear a helmet and gloves to protect her aura. He convinced his followers that Emmanuelle had supernatural powers and could move things with her mind. Before she entered a room, she yelled, "Ouvrez!" (open in french) and DiMambro pushed a button concealed beneath his cloak. The door opened, and his followers believed it was Emmanuelle opening the door with her mind. This was just another trick to keep his followers thinking that his family had special powers.

In March 1993, the Solar Temple became headline news in Canada when three members, including prophet Jouret, were arrested for trying to buy three guns with silencers. The Royal Canadian Mounted Police (RCMP), equivalent to the FBI in the United States, tapped the Temple's phone lines. They started investigating them for making threatening calls to members of the Canadian National Assembly (Quebec's provincial legislature), planning to bomb First Nations reserves and releasing explosions at Hydro Quebec transmission towers, the very business that employed Jouret to give motivational speeches to its employees.

Cult members, Jouret, Hermann Delorme, and Jean-Pierre Vinet, were convicted and fined for the gun charges. Jouret left Canada and went to Europe, never to return. At this point, the two leaders, Jouret and DiMambro, began to move in different directions in their respective lives.

On October 5, 1994, a farmhouse located in the town of Cheiry, Switzerland, caught on fire. When firefighters put the fire out and searched the house, they found the body of businessman, Albert Giacobino; only, it was a mystery because the man died from being shot. Investigators also discovered the farmhouse converted into a temple, with a pulpit and a pentagram drawn on the floor. Hanging over the pulpit was a picture of Jesus holding a chalice, but over the face of Jesus was one of Luc Jouret.

Around the base of the pulpit, arranged in a sunburst design, were 23 dead bodies, consisting of 10 men and 12 women, including DiMambro's 12year-old daughter. The men were all wearing white, black, and red robes, while the women had white and gold robes on. There were empty champagne bottles throughout the farm.

Half of the bodies had plastic bags wrapped over their heads and faces. Some of them had their hands tied behind their backs. A few of the bodies had been shot, some of them up to 8 times, all with a .22 caliber pistol. There were more than 50 shell casings on the floor beside the bodies.

Records later showed that there was a mayor, journalist, and civil servant found among the dead.

Many of the cultist's bodies were burnt so severely that coroners had to use dental records to identify the bodies. Many questions loomed. Such as, was this a mass murder or mass suicide?

Meanwhile, about fifty miles away in Granges-sur-Salvan, three chalets were burning. Inside the chalets were 25 bodies, 5 of them children, all of them badly burned. None of these victims were shot, but they did have plastic bags over their heads.

The remains showed that a few of them had been beaten badly, and most of them were heavily sedated before they were killed. The .22 caliber pistol used in the killings in the farmhouse was found on the floor of the chalet. Some of the members that died in these fires left suicide notes. All claimed that they were leaving this world to escape the hypocrisies and oppression.

Later that same day, a house in Quebec, owned by the Solar Temple, exploded. In the bedroom, the fireman found the bodies of a man and a woman. Both were wearing medallions with a double-headed eagle around their neck, which would only belong to members of the Solar Temple.

In the basement, a fireman found DiMambro's Swiss chauffeur, Tony Dutoit, his wife, and the body of their 3-month-old son, Emmanuel. The child was wedged behind a heater with a plastic bag tied over his head and a wooden stake through his heart. They had all been killed long before the fire was started. The fire had been started by a timer set to ignite cans of gasoline.

Investigators later discovered that according to cult

members, DiMambro said the chauffeur and his wife had the boy without his permission and believed the child to be the anti-Christ. He thought the boy was born into the cult to stop DiMambro's spiritual quest, so ordered to have him killed.

There were rumors all over the media that both DiMambro and Jouret escaped with 90 million pounds in a Swiss bank account and were living a life of luxury somewhere in the World. However, dental records later proved that DiMambro and Jouret were among the dead in the Chalet fires.

They were telling their followers that the end was coming very soon, and two days before the fires, took 12 members of the cult to a very expensive 'Last Supper.' DiMambro and Jouret believed that to be reborn on a different planet called Sirius, they had to go through a fiery death on Earth.

In December of 1995, sixteen cult members of the Solar Temple were found dead in Grenoble, France. In March of 1997, five more members were found burned to death in the house owned by Solar Temple in St. Casimir, Quebec.

One thing in common with all of these suicide murders was that they all occurred on the same dates of the annual equinoxes or solstices. Many letters were sent out to government agencies and media groups describing their deaths as a transition to the 'Dog Star' Sirius.

Michel Tabachnik, an internationally renowned Swiss conductor, was arrested as one of the leaders of the Solar Temple in the late 1990s. The charges against him included participation in the criminal organization and murder. The trial was held in Grenoble, France, during the spring of 2001, but he was acquitted. The French prosecutors appealed the decision, and the appellant court ordered a second trial. The second trial began in October of 2006 and lasted two months, but again he was found not guilty.

A search of DiMambro's mansion after his death found four red Ferraris and a Lamborghini. DiMambro and Jouret ended up owning at least 60 properties on three continents.

The core members of the group believed themselves to be a chosen people who were reincarnated periodically on Earth since ancient times to fulfill a cosmic mission. They gathered together for that purpose and were ready to sacrifice their lives for its sake, especially toward the end. Internal texts disclose these grandiose perspectives:

> "Do you understand what we represent? We are the promise that the Rosy Cross made to the Immutable. We are the Star Seeds that guarantee the perennial existence of the universe; we are the hand of God that shapes creation. We are the Torch that Christ must bring to the Father to feed the Primordial Fire and to reanimate the forces of Life, which, without our contribution, would slowly but surely go out. We hold the key to the universe and must secure its eternity."

IS THERE MORE TO COME?

The Order of the Solar Temple had a following in Spain, especially in the Canary Islands. In 1984, the founder of the OTS, Luc Jouret, lectured on the island of Tenerife.

The leader of the branch in Spain lived on the south part of the island. The only Spaniard who died in the suicides of the OTS was a barber from Tenerife. In 1998, a sect was suspected of plotting ritual suicide in the Teide National Park. Both Spanish and German police initially linked the group to the Order of the Solar Temple.

5

HEAVEN'S GATE

"We do in all honesty hate this world." - Marshall Applewhite

---

In March 1997, Marshall Applewhite, leader of the Heaven's Gate Cult, led 38 of his followers into mass suicide. Applewhite convinced his followers that their bodies were just containers for their souls, and for their

souls to be free, they would have to kill themselves. Once their souls were free, they would be transported to an alien craft that was going to pass the planet Earth at the same time as Comet Hale-Bopp.

Marshall Applewhite was the son of a Presbyterian minister. From a young age, he had homosexual feelings that his family wouldn't accept. In the 1970s, after a tremendous amount of pressure from his father, he checked himself into a mental hospital located in Houston, Texas, where he asked them to cure him of his homosexual feelings.

During his quest to cure himself of his sexuality, he met a nurse, Bonnie Lu Nettles, and they became a couple. The two decided to set up a group in California called the "Human Individual Metamorphosis."

It was Applewhite and Nettles' claim that they were sent to Earth by a spaceship to teach humans how to attain a level of consciousness beyond what was available here. The couple supported themselves and their new cult by stealing cars and committing credit card fraud.

After no success in California, they decided to move back to Texas. Applewhite took out a full-page advertisement that invited people to join their UFO club. Those who responded to the ad was sent a video showing Applewhite with two of his followers listening intently to every word Applewhite spoke.

Upon joining the group, you were required to give up your name, property, as well as become celibate. Applewhite and some of his senior lieutenants had themselves castrated.

In the ad published in *UFO Magazine*, Applewhite and Nettles used their new names, "Do" and "Ti." It was suggested that the names were taken from the notes in the musical scale (Do, Re, Mi, Fa, La, Ti, Do) used as the alien alert notes in the movie *Close Encounters of the Third Kind*.

Another suggestion to explain the names was that Applewhite had a special affection for the movie *The Sound of Music*, where the tea in that film was like the poison that cult members later took, which would take you back to Do. Other cult members had the names 'Re,' 'So,' and 'Fa.'

The cult created a screenplay which outlined its primary beliefs called *Beyond Human: Return of the Next Level*. A couple of tv networks were interested in making it into a movie, but it never happened.

Heaven's Gate moved from Arizona to San Diego and bought a $1.3 million mansion, which was once the residence of Douglas Fairbanks Jr. The property was on a hilltop and sat on three acres. None of the cult members would interact with their new neighbors.

They all slept in bunk beds and were not allowed to smoke or drink alcohol. The group was told not to have any contact with their families or old friends that were not in the group. The members earned money by designing websites. The website business was called "Higher Source" and had clients such as the San Diego Polo Club. Cult members also wore name badges that said they were the "Heaven's Gate Away Team." They considered themselves an 'away' team because they had been sent to Earth from another planet.

They also considered their bodies as merely a shell,

like a caterpillar, which would eventually shed its old shell and be reborn into a butterfly. The comet, Hale-Bopp, was deemed to be the sign of letting them know it was time to go home. They believed that behind the comet was a spacecraft sent to take them back home.

They announced their departure on their internet website:

> "RED ALERT – Hale-Bopp brings closure to Heaven's Gate."

Applewhite also wrote,

> "I am in the same position in today's society as was the One that was in Jesus then. If you want to go to Heaven, I can take you through that gate, but it requires everything from you."

Applewhite figured the approach of the comet Hale-Bopp meant that his 22 years of giving lessons to followers here on planet Earth were finally ending. He was graduating from the Human Evolutionary Level. He was delighted to leave this world and go with the spaceship crew.

According to Heaven's Gate, once an individual has perfected himself by following the "process," there were four ways to enter or "graduate" to the next level:

- Physical pickup onto a TELAH spacecraft and transfer to a next level body aboard that craft. In this version, what Professor Zeller calls a "UFO" version of the "Rapture," an alien spacecraft would descend to Earth, collect Applewhite, Nettles, and their followers, and their human bodies would be transformed through biological and chemical processes to perfected beings. This and other UFO-related beliefs held by the group have led some observers to characterize the group as a type of UFO religion;
- Natural death, accidental death, or death from random violence. Here, the "graduating soul" leaves the human container for a perfect next-level body;
- Outside persecution that leads to death. After the deaths of the Branch Davidians in Waco, Texas, and the events involving Randy Weaver at Ruby Ridge, Applewhite was afraid the American government would murder the members of Heaven's Gate;
- Willful exit from the body in a dignified manner. Near the end, Applewhite had a revelation that they might have to abandon their human bodies and achieve the next level as Jesus had done. This occurred on March 22 and 23, when 39 members died by suicide and "graduated."

Also, on the group's website, there were warnings that the planet Earth was about to be recycled. It stated that the only chance to survive was to leave with them on the spaceship. The cult prepared for their departure from Earth and sent their former members videos explaining what they were planning on doing. In the video, Applewhite said,

> "By the time you get this, we'll be gone, several dozens of us. We came from the Level Above Human in distant space, and we have now exited the bodies that we were wearing for our earthly task, returning to our world from whence we came, task completed."

Another cult member stated on the same video,

> "We couldn't be happier for what we're about to do."

A female cult member said,

> "Maybe they're crazy for all I know, but I don't have any choice but to go for it, because I've been on this planet for thirty-one years and there's nothing here for me."

After learning Applewhite had terminal cancer, another female cult member said,

---

> "Once he is gone, there is nothing left here on the face of the Earth for me, no reason to stay a moment longer."

Throughout the video, all 39 members would appear, having cut their hair short, which made them look like young men. Applewhite created a second video, where he tried to explain the group's beliefs.

> "We came for the express purpose to offer a doorway to the Kingdom of Heaven at the end of this civilization, the end of the millennium. Your only chance to evacuate is to leave with us. I guess we take the prize of the cult of cults."

Once the videos were sent, the 39 members went out for one final dinner at a local restaurant. When they returned from dinner, they broke into three groups and committed suicide over the next three days.

Applewhite had written out suicide instructions for each member. They were told to mix the phenobarbitone, a narcotic and sedative used to treat epilepsy, with pudding or apple sauce. They were to drink that with a vodka mixture and relax.

This method was ineffective, and most of the cult

members ended up dying of suffocation, and two of those members had to suffocate themselves.

A copy of the videos was sent to a Beverly Hills businessman who once employed one of the cult members. After watching them, he and another person drove to the San Diego mansion, where they found the 39 cult members all lying on their beds, dead. They all had their hands to their sides and faced the ceiling. They seemed to be staring through a three-foot square piece of purple silk, which was folded into a triangle pointing downwards. They each were wearing black pants and running shoes. Each of them had packed a bag as if they were going to travel somewhere. In each bag were the member's identification and a change of clothes.

The businessman called the police to the residence. The first two deputies that went near the bodies had to be rushed to the hospital, overcome from noxious fumes coming from the remains. A hazardous materials team was sent in to remove the bodies with a fork-lift and they were sent to the morgue in refrigerated trucks.

Applewhite's suicide note read

> "Two thousand years ago, a crew of members of the Kingdom of Heaven who are responsible for nurturing 'gardens,' determined that a percentage of the human 'plants' of the present civilization of this Garden (earth) had developed enough that some of those bodies might be ready to be used as 'containers' for soul deposits. Upon instruction, a member of the Kingdom of Heaven then left behind His body in that Next Level (similar to putting it in

a closet, like a suit of clothes that doesn't need to be worn for a while), came to earth, and moved into (or incarnated into), an adult human body (or 'vehicle') that had been 'prepped' for his particular task. The body that was chosen was called Jesus."

It has to be said that with the Heaven's Gate cult, much of their lifestyle was like what we have seen in science fiction movies or television series, including the way they dressed, how they behaved, their communications, and even their philosophy.

One of the most famous people that not only joined the cult but committed suicide with the other 38 people was Thomas Nichols, the brother of Nichelle Nichols, who starred on TV's Star Trek as Lt. Uhuru. The influences of Star Trek and Star Wars was even apparent in a member's speech in one of the suicide videos. The member was known as Stmody:

"We watch a lot of Star Trek, a lot of Star Wars, it's just like going on a holodeck. We've been in an astronaut training program. We figured out a day equals one thousand years and played it out mathematically. It's roughly thirty minutes. We've been training on a holodeck for thirty minutes. Now it's time to stop and put it to practice what we've learned. So, we take off the virtual reality helmet. We 'take off 'the vehicle that we've used for this

> task. We just set it aside, go back out of the holodeck to reality to be with the other members in the craft, in the heavens."

This statement made me believe that they saw themselves as space travelers in a science fiction program. So much so that they referred to themselves as the 'Away Team.'

When they found the 39 suicide members, they were dressed in uniforms of black shirts that displayed a triangular patch with "Heaven's Gate Away Team" written on it. The patches resembled the ones seen on the Starship Enterprise uniforms worn on their science fiction television program.

They also wore black pants and shoes. The shoes were Nike, which had the comet logo trademark. Heaven's Gate seamstresses made their uniforms. The cult also called their kitchens "nutrilabs" and the food preparations "experiments."

In an interview on January 22, 1994, an ex-cult member named Sawyer made comments that referred to the group as space travelers.

> "If you are on a spacecraft and you're performing tasks that are very important, let's say that you're designing a new physical vehicle for a soul to occupy, you have to have set guidelines for what you have to do. You can't go into that laboratory, any more than you can in chemistry class and

> design it yourself. And so, you learn the disciplines of following instructions."

I believe it was their science fiction-themed lifestyle that attracted new members. The members all described themselves as believers of UFOs, alien abductions, space aliens, and cattle mutilations. They also believed the world's governments were suppressing the truth from its citizens.

HALE-BOPP COMET

Alan Hale and Thomas Bopp discovered the Hale-Bopp comet separately on July 23, 1995. It became visible to the naked eye for about 18 months, starting in May 1996. The last time a comet drew this kind of attention was in 1811 when the "Great Comet of 1811" stayed visible for about nine months.

Hale-Bopp showed two gas trails, the blue trail was pointed straight away from the Sun, and the yellowish trail curved away along its orbit.

The comet also had a third tail that was only visible with telescopes, which was a sodium tail.

The comet was closest to the Earth on March 22, 1997 until it passed on April 1, 1997. It shone brighter than any other star in the sky except for Sirius, and its tails stretched 40-45 degrees across the sky. The comet was so bright that you could see it in the daytime. The last reported sighting of the comet was in December of 1997, which meant that it was visible to the naked eye for 569 days.

The last time the comet was thought to be seen was

during the Pharaoh Pepi's reign in Egypt in 2215 BC. Pepi's pyramid in Saqqara contains text referring to the comet as the "Nhh-star" and called it a companion to the pharaohs in heaven. "Nhh" is the hieroglyph for long hair. It was also thought to have almost collided with Jupiter during its 2215 BC pass through the Solar System, close enough to have changed the planet's gravity.

The comet is still being observed by astronomers and will be until 2020 when it is no longer trackable. The comet is estimated to return in the year 4385. The estimated probability of Hale-Bop striking Earth in the future pass is remote, but as in previous passes through the solar system, the comet's trajectory could be changed. The comet has a 60 kilometer diameter, and the consequences of something that large either hitting or passing close to the Earth would be apocalyptic.

The comet created a considerable amount of UFO claims after an amateur astronomer Chuck Shramek of Houston, Texas, took an image of the comet that showed a fuzzy, slightly long object close to it. Shramek called into the national talk show Art Bell's Coast to Coast, to report what he saw. He described it as a 'Saturn-like object' that was following the comet. UFO believers thought it was an alien spacecraft following the comet, and even remote viewers like Courtney Brown admitted that she could see it was an alien spacecraft. Art Bell claimed to have obtained an image of the spacecraft from an astrophysicist, who was about to confirm the discovery. However, astronomers Oliver Hainaut and David Tholen of the University of Hawaii stated that the photo was an altered copy of one of their comet images.

Nancy Lieder, a computer professional, author, and

founder of the website ZetaTalk, claims to receive messages from aliens through an implant in her brain, said that Hale-Bopp was just a fictional design created to distract the people from the soon to arrive planet, Nibiru. Also called Planet X, Nibiru, is supposed to be an invisible planet that will pass by Earth and disrupt the Earth's rotation, thereby causing a global cataclysm. Lieder's original date for this to happen was in May of 2003, and then later, she tied it to the 2012 phenomenon. In both cases, it never happened, but vast amounts of people with websites and Facebook groups continue to predict the coming of Nibiru.

6

BRANCH DAVIDIANS

"If the Bible is true, then I'm Christ." - David Koresh

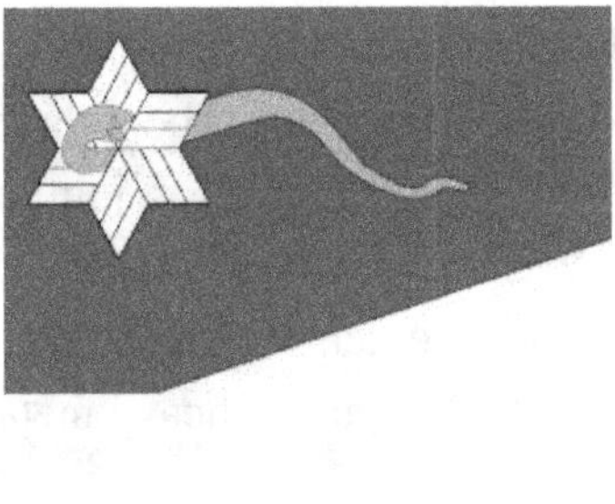

UNDER ANY OTHER NAME, IT'D BE OKAY!

Victor Houteff was an immigrant to America from Bulgaria. He was a Seventh Day Adventist preacher until the year 1930 when he was defrocked for heresy. After he left the church, he decided to start his own sect and called it the "Davidians," after the biblical King David.

Houteff claimed that he had uncovered a hidden code within the Bible, which revealed impending doom and even the end of the world. He also claimed that God had chosen him to lead a group of people that would rule the Earth alongside Jesus Christ.

Houteff set up a school at Mount Carmel, near Waco, Texas, where he taught his interpretations of the scriptures.

When he died, Benjamin Roden took over the group and renamed it the "Branch" after an apocalyptic verse in the Bible. Unlike Houteff, Roden didn't set a date for the second coming or end of the World.

The church, under its new leadership, took on a more conspiratorial view of the World, and its members handed out pamphlets explaining their weird beliefs. One such brochure described how the Pope had masterminded Watergate against thenPresident Nixon.

In 1978, Benjamin Roden died, and his wife, Lois Roden, took over the leadership. About three years into her reign, she allowed Vernon Howell to join the cult. Howell was a 23-year-old man born illegitimately to a 14-year-old schoolgirl. He had problems learning at school, so he dropped out in grade 9 to pursue heavy metal guitaring and bodybuilding.

Howell begged Lois to join the group. He was an excessive masturbator and wanted her help dealing with his issue.

Howell became quite popular with the other members of the group. He was a capable handyman and could fix all the issues they had with their buildings at Mt. Carmel.

Howell knew the whole New Testament by heart and was able to talk scripture, which mesmerized the group, and after a while they became more like followers than co-members.

Howell approached Lois, who was now 70 years-old and told her that God had decreed the two of them have a child together. Even though her age precluded any real possibility of conception, they did become lovers.

Howell began to give sermons that have been described as hellfire-and-damnation rants, convincing the Branch Davidians that the apocalypse was at hand and that it was time to follow him as the new prophet. He pushed Lois aside and married a 14-year-old girl from the cult. Howell claimed it was up to him to have sex with as many girls as possible, which included girls that were as young as 12 years old.

Lois expelled Howell from the cult, along with his wife and new-born child. Howell left with 25 other members that wanted to continue following him, and at first, they traveled around America's Midwest. After no success in finding a good location to relocate, the group moved to Palestine, where his status of a prophet was confirmed. He claimed he was the chosen one to fight the World's last great battle against Satan.

Howell traveled to Australia, where he was able to recruit more members, but eventually relocated the whole cult back to America. He settled in Texas with 60 followers. Most of the people he converted were musicians or bodybuilders. His inner circle was all bodybuilders he called 'The Mighty Men.' Howell, like Charles Manson, believed he saw hidden messages from God encoded in rock songs, one such song was *House of the Rising Sun* by The Animals.

When Howell thought his group was ready, he attacked the Branch Davidians compound in Waco and shot their new leader, George Roden, Lois' son, and successor. Howell and his Mighty Men were arrested and charged with the shooting but were later acquitted and released from prison. He returned to the Davidian ranch and expelled Lois. He took over as the new cult leader, which now had well over 100 members.

A NEW BEGINNING

Vernon Howell changed his name to David Koresh, taking his first name from King David and the second from the Hebrew name of the Babylonian King Cyrus, who had allowed the exiled Jews to return to Palestine.

The compound at Waco was now renamed, the "Ranch Apocalypse," as it was now considered to be the place where the battle of Armageddon would happen. The Branch Davidians were also renamed "The Army of God."

The cult started to amass a vast arsenal of weapons, including hand grenades and anti-tank guns. The group lived under Martial Law, and the rules were strictly enforced. Koresh would not allow any sort of dissent and took care of the troublemakers without question.

Koresh took his pick of wives and daughters from his followers, some of them underage, but he had sex with them regardless.

Meanwhile, the other men in the group were denied sex and told by Koresh that they had to save themselves for battle.

Mark Breault, one of Koresh's original Mighty Men, was unhappy in the group after his wife left to return to Australia. He eventually left the group as well, taking with him his diary of the days he spent with Koresh. He went to the authorities and warned them that Waco was going to be another Jonestown. However, law enforcement didn't start to investigate the group for another two years.

On February 28, 1993, officers from the Bureau of Alcohol, Tobacco and Firearms (ATF) decided to move in on the Branch Davidians in response to complaints of them stockpiling illegal firearms and sexual assaults on minors. There has been much controversy about whether the ATF had the authority to move in on the compound in Waco or not.

The operation was supposed to be secret, but during the setup, the ATF stumbled across a reporter and told him what they were doing. It was leaked back to the compound, and the members were prepared for the attack.

Upon arriving at the compound under a disguise concealed in cattle trailers, they rushed out but were met with gunfire. The battle lasted just under one hour. Four ATF agents were killed, and 24 others were injured. The Davidians lost six members.

The Federal Bureau of Investigation (FBI) took over the operation. It brought in their hostage negotiators, who were only trained to deal with criminal gangs and politically motivated terrorists, not religious groups. The public was surprised and embarrassed by the incompetence of the ATF. The entire country watched on live TV every day with 24 hour news coverage.

The negotiators had no understanding of the Book of Revelations and didn't listen to any of Koresh's ideas about the Fifth Seal, which was an enactment of mass suicide. Instead, they dismissed it and didn't believe the group had the same devotion as the People's Temple and Jim Jones.

The FBI was able to manage the situation at first and had some success when two older women and 21 children were allowed to leave the compound. This left about 100 members still inside, and at least 17 of them were children.

As the siege continued, the FBI decided to employ psychological tactics on the group. Spotlights were directed at all the windows, to try and disrupt the member's sleep. Loudspeakers were set up around the compound with the chanting of Tibetan monks, screams of dying rabbits, and loud rock music playing constantly.

The Branch Davidians darkened their windows with blankets to try and block the bright lights and piled bales of hay against the walls to try and deaden the sounds coming from the speakers. These tactics went on for weeks without any breaks, and people from around the world could watch it live on cable news.

After several weeks of having no success, Attorney General Janet Reno sought permission from then-President Bill Clinton, to have the FBI use tear gas to flush out the Davidians and save the children that were being held in the compound.

At 4 a.m. on April 19, 1993, after 51 days of siege, two tanks fitted with battering rams moved into position outside of the compound. Over the loudspeakers, the FBI announced they wanted the Davidians to come out with their hands above their heads, and nobody would be harmed.

Instead, the Davidians fired on the tanks in order to

stop them. But the tanks were able to plow through the compound walls and pump tear-gas into the buildings. The Davidians even had gas masks to help them with this possibility.

Around noon that same day, FBI overheard plans that the Davidians were going to set the compound on fire, and later saw smoke. The wind was strong that day, and in an instant, the ranch was engulfed in flames. It wasn't long before the ranch tower collapsed, and the ammunition storage went up in a series of massive explosions.

Eight members of the cult managed to escape from the burning buildings, but over 100 people died that day. The bodies of 25 children were later discovered. Twelve of them were David Koresh's children. All of them were burned, but some also had other types of wounds. There was a two-year-old boy who had been stabbed several times and a woman that had been shot in the back.

Seventeen more bodies were discovered with gunshot wounds, five of them children that Koresh had shot through the forehead. Koresh was shot and killed by one of his aides, who then shot himself.

Kathryn Schroder was one of the survivors who testified that the Davidians had always planned to kill anyone that tried to attack the compound. Eleven of the other survivors were charged with conspiracy and murder. A jury later found that the ATF was also responsible for the deaths of their agents because of the way that they conducted the raid on the compound. Five of the Davidians were found guilty of involuntary manslaughter, and two others were convicted of firearms charges, while four were found innocent of all charges.

If you get a chance to read a book written by one of the

survivors, David Thibodeau, called *Waco: A Survivor's Story*, do so. It's a great read, and you'll hear details of what happened to the victims before, during, and after their ordeal with the cult.

THE MAURY POVICH SHOW

After being invited, some survivors decided to go on *The Maury Povich Show* to tell their story. Here is an excerpt from Thibodeau's book, which describes how the Waco survivors were set up on the show when they tried to explain exactly what happened, and why they chose to not only live on the compound, but to stand with Koresh and risk their own lives:

> "Why didn't they just let the children go?" shouted a redhead sitting right behind me, and the audience cheered her roundly. This person, who pretended to be an audience member, was actually an attendant on Povich's flight to Waco. She, too, had been seen backstage consulting over a script, and all through the taping she leaped to her feet with the same shout — "What about the kids?" Every time Balenda and Mark (two of the survivors of Waco) tried to turn the focus back to the government's actions, the audience started screaming about the children. "Why didn't you guys come out with a kid under each arm? "No-one wanted to leave," Catherine Matteson explained, but she was hooted down. Balenda fought like a tigress against the rising tide of malice, refusing to shut up at Povich's

> command. "Balenda, this is not your show, this is my show," the famous host said testily. She was often booed and rarely applauded by the studio crowd. When Mark tried to say that we should put our raw emotions aside for a moment and dispassionately consider the facts, the audience hissed him into silence. "It was like being eaten alive on television," Balenda said afterward, tears of frustration in her eyes."

Author's Note: Is live talk shows truly the way we want to get our information now? Or is this the modern way we publicly shame those in our society when we don't agree? It is, after all, a commercial market. We paid for the cable, which paid the network or channel for a show, which chose people for those shows that would provide the highest entertainment value, so we will keep on paying. On shows like Maury Povich, we get to call his guests names and attack their motives, just to make us feel better than them. But we paid for it, right?

I can't help but wonder what's next. Will we start to bring back public executions like pay-per-view sporting events? There is a resurgence of crime television, podcasts and books out there that are no longer held to any kind of standard. Next up, the return of Court TV, streaming on a website, or smart tv near you! Maybe the total distrust in the justice system to hold a fair trial will lead people to not only want to watch a trial on television but vote on it too. It would be kind of a new version of the X-Factor or America's Got Talent.

I know my sarcasm is palpable; however, I would never have chosen an outlet like Maury Povich. I like the guy. If you've ever met him, he is a super person to be around. But his show is what it is – a program that runs on ratings resulting from the amount of excitement and drama that occurs during the hour-long episodes. The more excitement, screaming and fighting, the better the show's ratings. When a show's attitude is to have a lie detector episode to prove who the baby's daddy is, then being in a terrible, tragic, and complicated situation such as the Waco siege, could only end in devastation.

I don't say this to insult or judge the survivors of Waco, who did choose to participate in the show. They could not have known that they were going to be set up. Not only were there the typical stupid rants and name-calling from the real audience but there were also actors hired by the television show to create drama, cause fights, and ask questions that put the survivors in a terrible light. After all, what kind of person goes to this type of show? And why are they going? To scream and say mean things, wear funny clothes, a chance to be seen on tv, or, even better, to talk to Maury.

MANDELA EFFECT?

Do you ever have those moments when you enter your bedroom to get something, and you can't remember what it was you came in for in the first place? It seems to become more frequent as we get older. Or when someone tells a group of friends a story about something that happened to them, and after a few tellings of the same story, certain things change? This happens because our brains have several parts that hold different pieces of memory. So, when all parts are functioning, the memory is complete. But sometimes over the years, things happen to certain parts of the brain, which causes it not to remember the whole story correctly. So, what does the brain do to compensate? It fills in the blank spots with the knowledge it has acquired over our years of living in our world.

Recently the idea of 'time slips' or false memories has been dubbed "The Mandela Effect" by pseudo-scientists. It's hard to believe that we actually have some people who prefer to look to pseudoscience for answers to the unexplained, but the fact that some believe the unbelievable is the basis of this book.

Instead of the rational explanation that different parts of our brain are not working in sync, thereby causing memory blocks, some would rather believe that something somewhere just stopped time, went back and changed some event, then returned to the present time. This is, in essence, the Mandela Effect, and it comes from when Nelson Mandela died, there were several people who claimed they remembered him dying years ago.

I only bring this effect into the conversation because of its relation to the subject of the book, cults. When we have people believing there is an afterlife, a god, and create a religion around it, then try to live by it, that will be the formula by which they live the rest of their lives unless there is a major change.

Would this Mandela Effect not be a belief – a faith of some sort that something much larger than us is in control?

Let's take that analogy and apply it to a situation. Say, for instance, there's a group of us all taking part in a play. We each have our roles to play in the show, and when we play these roles, we draw from all the information we have accumulated over our lives. Actors will play the same role quite differently because they've lived different lives.

Now ten years pass by since our group performed that play, and we have a reunion. Unfortunately, one of the actors died a few years back, so we are one short in the reunion. When we want to retell the story of our group putting on that play ten years ago, one part of the memory is now missing. So, what does the group do? The same thing our brain does in this situation. It fills in the blanks from the knowledge we have accumulated over our lives.

This 'filling in the blanks' of memory recall is the main reason that 75% of eyewitness testimonies are not reliable. It's not that the witness is untrustworthy or trying to deceive the police. It's simply that they only have what information their brain supplies when they try to recall it.

COULD IT HAPPEN AGAIN?

On April 19, 1995, when the Oklahoma City bombing occurred on the second anniversary of the siege at Waco, it was in retaliation. The Branch Davidians continues to operate to this day. One member who was not at the compound during the raid is still awaiting Koresh's resurrection. Another member that lost his son, two daughters, and four grandchildren during the attack still believes Koresh's prophecy of the second coming will come true.

Today, a church stands where the remaining Branch Davidians worship. It was built on top of the foundation where the original building burned. Videographer Dan Bell who filmed the compound in 2016, commented,

"It's very strange that there are still Branch Davidians

living here. They still kind of worship David Koresh. It's very kind of unnerving when you're there, to think these people cannot see how he was wrong."

Fortunately, the people still there aren't as organized as they were in 1993.

7

THE MANSON FAMILY

"I'm Jesus Christ, whether you want to accept it or not, I don't care." - Charles Manson

---

Ever since Charles Manson was remanded into state prison on April 22, 1971, for seven counts of first degree murder and one count of conspiracy to commit murder, he has remained the real-life face of the 'Boogeyman.'

How did someone like Manson hold that title for so many years, even while locked up in a high security prison, until his death recently in 2017? There have been so many other murderers in America, that have done so much worse, and to so many more people. My statement doesn't mean to lessen the real evil of Manson to any degree. It merely means to delve deeper and to question what it is that holds one person out among the others.

Some people claim it's the way that he killed his victims. But since the 1960s, home invasions have not gotten any 'nicer.' I could show you many examples of torture inflicted on innocent people and children in their own homes, and chances are you wouldn't remember the killer in those crimes.

Some say that it's because Manson was so smart, devious, and had an evil piercing look in his eyes that made your skin crawl. I agree with those statements about Manson, but Richard Rodriguez reeked of what the boogeyman would look like just as much.

Maybe it was just the intense level of terror Manson could subject anyone to, anywhere, anytime, that added not only the fear of what he could do to you physically but mentally as well. He was able to leave you feeling defenseless to his every thought.

Like the other true accounts in this book, I wanted to delve into the details of how the mind works when it comes to cults. You can find much more detailed reports on the Manson Family crimes, but here the point is to determine why people not only followed a cult or cult leader like Charles Manson but why did they kill for him?

BACKGROUND

This story all started in the 1960s when the counterculture was looking for something different from how their parents lived their lives. The idea of God was still okay to the youth, but they wanted to experience more love and closeness amongst themselves. Affection was not something their parents displayed in public; after all, that would be a sin against God.

The youth of that time were looking for more freedom. Not only the freedom from their parent's idea of traditional living: going to work, having a family, paying bills, painting the house or cutting the lawn in their only free time, doing whatever your neighbors were doing, obtaining the latest item was advertised on your television, etc.

They wanted the freedom to express themselves in their love for each other, a more spiritual path than the one their parents took. They desired the freedom to live a lifestyle that wasn't accepted within their parent's version of God. So they reached out and found an alternative spirituality that would allow both.

In the 1960s, along came several versions of existing churches that opened their doors to others that were uncomfortable being themselves in their current venue. It's necessary to understand that it was still very important for the young counterculture to still have God included in their lives; they just wanted to change the rules they had been taught.

New rules began to permeate the country, and Charles Manson and his family were only one of the hundreds popping up around this time. By the mid-sixties, Timothy Leary, an American psychologist and advocate for psychedelic drugs who spoke to crowds of up to 30,000 people, dubbed this new era, "Turn on, tune in, drop out." The country started to see the rise of the 'hippies' in San

Francisco, who followed Leary's mantra. Their lifestyles involved alternative ways of dressing, healthier eating, more communal living, summers of love, and, most importantly, 'dropping out' of the political mainstream, believing the only way to make a change in society was to drop out altogether.

POPULAR DRUGS OF THE ERA AND EXPERIMENTS

The most popular drugs of this culture were marijuana and LSD. LSD was a significant drug for the 1960s for many reasons. For the youth of the counterculture, the use of LSD was purported to help them evolve and expand their spirituality and religious experiences. It would help them understand their lives more fully. The effects of drugs were quite mystical and resulted in the users seeing different colors and more.

Popular rock groups of the day, such as the Grateful Dead, Pink Floyd, Jimi Hendrix, the Byrds, and Janis Joplin were all using LSD openly, which in turn helped it to gain even more popularity among the suburban teenagers.

The use of LSD caught the attention of the United States Government and Military, but for different reasons. After its discovery in November 1938 by Swiss scientist Albert Hofmann, it was originally intended to be used as a respiratory and circulatory stimulant in the 1940s and 1950s. It was placed on hold when World War II started and the focus of pharmaceutical companies changed. Five years later, Hofmann decided he would go back to work with the idea and he resynthesized it. During this second experiment with LSD, Hofmann absorbed some of it on his hands and later found himself at home in a state of intoxication.

Two days later, on April 19, 1943, Hofmann performed an experiment on himself to determine what the exact effects of LSD were. Intentionally, he ingested 250 micrograms of the substance. In less than an hour, Hofmann began to sweat profusely, so he decided to ride his bicycle home and rest. Hofmann's condition accelerated into heavy breathing and a rapid feeling of anxiety, where he started to believe his neighbor was a malevolent witch, he thought that he had gone insane, and the LSD had poisoned him. His family doctor came to Hofmann's house, and upon examination, found no physical abnormalities, except for extremely dilated pupils. After that, April 19 was and is still celebrated as "Bicycle Day" in psychedelic communities to commemorate Hofmann's first ride and the discovery of LSD.

In 1947, LSD was introduced and became a part of the American medical community because they believed LSD had some clinical applications. Throughout the 1950s, major medical centers began to experiment and even use LSD, believing it could be helpful in curing alcoholism, facilitating psychotherapy, and enhancing creativity. In the late 1950s, they gave LSD to 22 patients that had minor personality disorders. In another experiment by psychiatrist Oscar Janiger, they administered it to over 100 creative people, including writers, artists, composers, and poets, to see how much more creative they would be in their work.

In the 1950s, LSD became a media sensation in psychiatry, and they reported on many positive responses they discovered. In one case, Dr. Humphry Osmond gave LSD to alcoholics who were in Alcoholics Anonymous but were unable to quit drinking. After a year, about 50% of the study group had not had a drink of alcohol, a success rate that had never been seen before.

Overall, LSD was prescribed to over 40,000 patients during the 1950s and 1960s, including movie star Cary Grant who was one of many given the drug as part of their psychotherapy.

But as with all drugs designed to help make people feel better, LSD started getting used recreationally, and gaining a larger usage in the general population. It was the new celebrity designer 'drug of choice.' And it was making its rounds at all the Hollywood parties and within the counter-cultures that needed LSD to help them find a new level of spirituality.

There was also another group just as interested in the drug. Only they weren't making the media or attending parties. They were the United States' Central Intelligence Agency (CIA).

Project MKUltra was the code name given to a program of experiments on human subjects that were designed and undertaken by the CIA. The operation was officially sanctioned in 1953, and the experiments were intended to identify and develop drugs and procedures to be used in interrogations. They were seeking a drug that weakened an individual and forced their confession through mind control.

This program engaged in several illegal activities, including the use of U.S. and Canadian citizens as its unwitting test subjects, and the use of numerous methods that would manipulate people's mental states and alter brain functions. Those methods included administering high doses of LSD and other chemicals, electroshock therapy, hypnosis, sensory deprivation, isolation, verbal and sexual abuse, and other forms of torture.

The scope of this project was enormous for the time. *Project MKUltra* research was undertaken at 80 institutions, including colleges, universities, hospitals, prisons, and pharmaceutical companies. The CIA operated these projects under a front organization to keep it secret from the general public, workers, and students frequenting those places. Later it was discovered and revealed that top officials of those locations were aware of what the CIA was doing.

By the mid-1960s, the use of LSD was garnering lots of attention. It was perceived to have a negative effect on the values of the Christian middle class, who felt under attack by what they considered it to be the devil's drug. The backlash forced the government to restrict use of the drug by making it illegal. They declared it a Schedule 1 substance, thereby designating the drug as having a high potential for abuse, and lacking any currently accepted medical use in treatments.

Even with the major changes to the LSD drug laws in place, the CIA continued their experiments on people using the now illegal drug, and it was still available on the streets. Manson and his 'family' used it frequently.

After Manson was released from a Los Angeles prison in June 1967, he and his girls headed for San Francisco, for the summer of love. He rented an apartment across from a newly opened Haight Ashbury Free Medical Clinic (HAFMC). The clinic offered a free safe space for the homeless, addicted, or shamed kids that couldn't get medical care from regularly paid doctors.

The clinic helped poor people who couldn't afford medical exams or treatments and specialized in addiction treatments and sexual disease awareness. The clinic became a regular hang-out for Manson and his family, as the clinic would check them for STDs.

The clinic was founded by Dr. David Smith, a medical doctor, and researcher. Smith's research involved pumping lab rats full of speed as well as psychedelic drugs, like LSD and mescaline, and inducing aggressive states in them. The reason HAFMC could offer its services for free was because its operators were involved in federally-funded research.

Dr. Smith was involved in two federally funded studies: *The San Francisco Project*, a study on parole best practices, and the *Amphetamine Research Project (ARP)*, a study on the effects of speed on violent behavior in street gangs. Both of these projects were funded through the National Institute for Mental Health, which had been used as a front for CIA money during the MKULTRA psychedelic experiments. Another MKULTRA-funded project titled Mass Conversion used informants to infiltrate street gangs to engineer a shift in "basic moral, religious or political matters."

The most famous researcher working out of the HAFMC was Louis Jolyon West, a psychologist who was a contractor in the CIA's MKULTRA mind control experiments. West popped up in the background of some significant events in the 1960s and 1970s. He examined Lee

Harvey Oswald's assassin Jack Ruby, who mysteriously developed psychotic delusions immediately following West's visit.

West was brought in to cure Patty Hearst's Stockholm syndrome. He also famously killed an elephant with a cocktail of LSD and amphetamines while trying to induce a "must," an aggressive state that occurs during mating. But West first rose to prominence as a psychological expert called in to deprogram some Korean War POWs who were supposedly brainwashed into claiming the United States had committed war crimes.

Recently, author and researcher Tom O'Neill suggested in his book *Chaos: Charles Manson, the CIA, and the Secret History of the Sixties*, the possibility that Manson might have been a 'Manchurian Candidate,' a robot programmed by the state to do its dirty work. But he failed to prove it. Regardless, I would argue at the very least, Manson certainly learned the background behind the LSD drug, and the effects it could have on people, including hallucinations and believing in things that weren't true.

MANSON FAMILY LIFESTYLE

The Vietnam War continued to kill thousands, the civil rights movement was well underway, and Charles Manson, newly released from prison, was hitch-hiking his way to San Francisco with nothing but an acoustic guitar. It was truly fitting as the Bay area acted as the headquarters for young people aged 15 – 30 years-old, who couldn't relate to the ideals of the older generations. The youth of this time was not going to follow their parent's ways of wars and racism.

Manson had the hair, the guitar, and spoke the words the young wanted to hear, about peace and love. Manson later claimed that it was because he was the only one who told them the truth. These kids were running away from their parents that were either divorced or alcoholics, and they could no longer take the pressure of the lifestyle in which mainstream society was forcing them to live.

During these times, many groups were living transient lifestyles, with no real direction except to find love and spiritual development. Dianne 'Snake' Lake was a 14-year-old girl that joined the Manson Family in the later 1960s with permission from her parents. Snake, like many other young teenagers, had parents that decided to quit their jobs, sell their house and property, buy an old bread van, and turn it into a make-shift camper. Her parents were on a spiritual journey, so they climbed into their new home-made camper and headed on the road to nowhere.

> "They would go town to town, and flop at known hippie houses throughout California. Sometimes you would like the house and stay for months, other times only a couple of hours or a day, it all depended on the 'vibe man.'"

During this transient way of life, families would meet and get to know other families attempting to live the same free lifestyle and find heaven. Some families would exchange members with each other, knowing that they could meet up somewhere down the road on their journey.

Such was the case with Diane 'Snake' Lake. Her

family met Charles Manson on one of their journeys, and left Snake with him, as they wanted to travel a different direction at that time. Snake went with Manson. If you would like to hear about what a wild journey that was, read her book, *Members of the Family: My Story of Charles Manson, Life Inside His Cult, and the Darkness That Ended the Sixties*. It will give you a good understanding of the atmosphere in California in the 1960s.

The part of her book that stayed with me was the story of when Snake was traveling on a bus with Manson and a few other family members, and they were pulled over by the police. Nobody was arrested that day except for Snake. When the police asked everyone for their identification, they found out that she was only 14-years-old, so they took her to jail.

After arriving at the local police detachment, they finally located Snake's parents and told them they had to come to get their daughter. When the parents arrived, they got her out of the building and sent her off to where Charles Manson was waiting, parked across the street with his bus. This was the hippie life in the 1960s.

Leslie Van Houten, one of Manson's devoted followers, admitted that she was desperately seeking someone she could love, hold on to, and call her own. Van Houten also claimed that in the early days, when she first joined Charlie, it was fun and innocent, where everybody was happy to be alive.

Manson was mostly adding young females to his family. He looked for girls that were fairly attractive so he could use them to lure in some male followers too. One of the most well-known of these male followers is Charles 'Tex' Watson, who grew up in a religious household in

Copeville, Texas. Watson decided to leave his well-structured life at the University of Texas in the summer of 1967 to head for California.

Manson invited large numbers of young people to visit and stay with him. He gave them generous doses of LSD while taking only smaller amounts for himself. He encouraged group sex, saying that it was the only way to break down society's rigid, unnatural views of sexuality.

Manson found an old school bus and took his followers on trips to Los Angeles, where they dug through garbage bins to find food or steal what they could from suburban neighborhoods.

Manson and his family crashed wherever they could. One of his mainstays in 1967 and 1968 was at Brian Wilson's rented house in the Pacific Palisades area.

Within a year, though, he was kicked out by Wilson's manager. Manson and his followers found a new spot at the Spahn Ranch, a horse-and-ride-farm owned by George Spahn. Spahn was nearly blind and 80 years old, so he hired the Manson family to take care of the ranch, give horse rides, and cook for the crew. One of the extra benefits Manson gave Spahn was the use of one of his girls, Lynette 'Squeaky' Fromme, to help him see, but also to perform sexual duties upon request. Fromme later was imprisoned for attempting to kill President Gerald Ford.

The ranch was located about 30 miles from Los Angeles and fairly isolated, which made it easier for Manson to make it his kingdom. This was the perfect place to cut off his followers from the real world. The group lived like a real commune, sharing clothes when they weren't walking around naked, taking turns cooking and cleaning, and everyone doing any household chores that needed to be done.

They had lots of parties with copious amounts of LSD. They often engaged in group sex with each other, and with the new people that the girls lured to the ranch.

In November 1968, the Beatles released their ninth studio album, *The Beatles*, which is often referred to as the White Album. Many of the songs on the album were written during the band's trip to India, where they were studying Transcendental Meditation. The song "Helter Skelter," on side three of the double album, was a reference to an amusement park slide in Britain. Neither Manson nor the others were aware of the reference. But in Manson's mind, the lyrics of the song confirmed for him what he had suspected and what he had been teaching his followers – America was on the cusp of an apocalyptic race war between the whites and blacks. Armageddon was imminent, and he planned to survive it, along with his family, in a hideout in a Death Valley cave. So, Manson dubbed this Armageddon "Helter Skelter." Susan Atkins, one of Manson's top followers, described Helter Skelter as the last war that would ever happen on Earth.

After the murders, when the FBI interviewed Manson, he claimed the notion of Helter Skelter was a way for him to keep a tight grip on his followers.

Manson believed he was the son of God, hence his name "Man" and "Son." He often told his followers that he was Jesus Christ, who returned to govern the new world after the race war. Manson believed that the blacks would annihilate all of the whites, but they were not capable of governing themselves, never mind the world, so it was left to him.

HELTER SKELTER

On August 9, 1969, Tex Watson grabbed a gun, several knives, and a few of the Manson female followers, including Linda Kasabian, 20, pregnant, and the only family member that had a valid driver's license, ordering her to drive them to 10050 Cielo Drive. This was the home of Terry Melcher, Doris Day's son and famous music producer, and the same producer that decided not to sign Manson to a record contract. Melcher's business had taken him away from California for a while, so he leased out his house to movie director Roman Polanski and his movie star wife, Sharon Tate.

Polanski was away in London filming a new movie, leaving his 8-month pregnant wife alone in the house. Tate had her friends over for the night, including Jay Sebring, 35, Tate's former fiancé and men's hairstylist; Voytek Frykowski, 37, a writer and producer; and Abigail Folger, 26, the Folger Coffee heiress and social activist who was Frykowski's girlfriend. Frykowski and Folger were planning on staying at the house to make sure that Tate was okay until Polanski returned from his work in London.

After cutting the telephone line to the house, the Manson followers climbed the gate onto the property and started walking up the driveway towards the house.

Steven Parent, 18, was just leaving after visiting with the live-in caretaker. As he was driving his car out the driveway, he turned on his headlights and spotted the intruders walking up the driveway towards the house. He slowed his vehicle to a stop and rolled down the driver's side window to ask them what they were doing. Tex Watson approached the open car window, bent down, and shot Parent four times. Reaching into the car, he turned the car off. The timing of his death was estimated to be 12:15 a.m. because when Watson shot into the car, he hit the car radio and stopped the clock from working.

The Manson intruders cased the house looking for any unlocked doors or open windows, but there were none. Watson found a window that was open but had a locked screen on it. He sliced up the screen just enough for Susan Atkins, and Patricia Krenwinkel to get inside the house. Atkins went to the door and let Watson in.

The intruders rounded up all the people in the house and told them that they were going to die as they tied them up. Atkins grabbed Sharon Tate, who was resting in her room, dressed in a bra and bikini bottoms, and tied her up with a nylon rope thrown over a ceiling beam, with her arms held above her head.

Tate was pleading for her life and the life of her baby, "Please don't kill my baby! You can take me anywhere and let me have my baby. Then you can kill me." Susan Atkins firmly said, "Look, bitch, I have no mercy for you; you're going to die, and you better get used to it." Then Atkins stabbed Tate 16 times, including in the stomach.

The Manson attackers killed everyone in the house that night, one by one, stabbing them a collective 102 times, far more than necessary to kill them. Sebring died while holding his hands over his face.

Linda Kasabian stayed in the car as the lookout, and later testified in court that she heard so many screams coming from the house, she got out of the car and walked towards the house. She saw one of the victims, Frykowski, covered in blood, stumbling out the front door. Soon after, Watson followed, jumped onto Frykowski's back, and stabbed him until he stopped moving. Watson pulled out his gun and started beating the lifeless body over the head. Police found Frykowski still clutching the grass with his left fingers the next morning.

Abigail Folger made a run for it out the back door but was quickly caught by Patricia Krenwinkel, who tacked her on the lawn with her full body weight. Krenwinkel was so angry about Folger's escape that she stabbed her with intense rage. Folger died with her white nightgown turned to an almost solid red from her own blood.

Up to this night, Manson and his family had mainly committed crimes for money or valuables to live. But in this crime, there was nothing taken of any value from the house or the bodies. The last thing the Manson crew did was to take Sharon Tate's blood and write "pig" on the front door.

About 8:30 a.m. the following morning, Winifred Chapman, the housekeeper, came to do the job she did every day. She noticed the cut phone line, but that didn't stop her from entering the house. When she walked in, she noticed the place was in disarray and started to pick things up until she walked into the living room where Sharon Tate had been killed. She screamed aloud, turned around, and ran to the neighbors to call the police.

Upon entering the house, the police saw that the bodies were so badly beaten, with bloody faces, bullet wounds, and there was so much blood spread throughout the house that there was no need to check to see if any of the victims were alive. The authorities originally arrested the live-in caretaker William Garretson, who was taken in for questioning.

During the attacks, he claimed to be home but said he heard nothing because he had his music playing. He didn't notice anything unusual except that the phone line was dead. He was charged with the murders but released after he took a polygraph test and passed it. Polanski was told of the massacre while still in London filming his latest movie. He was distraught and booked the next flight home to Los Angeles.

Fear struck Hollywood quickly. All the newspapers ran headlines calling the murders, "Ritual Killings," or "Satanic Sacrifices." The rich and famous throughout Beverly Hills were buying guard dogs, guns, and hiring security staff. The Beverly Hills' gun stores sold over 200 guns on the following two days after the murders. Security company firms more than tripled their staff. Other big celebrities like Frank Sinatra just left town.

HELTER SKELTER – REDO

It was now time for Manson to implement the second night of Helter Skelter, but this time he would tag along for the killings. Manson wasn't pleased about the Cielo Drive murders, and he chastised his crew for being sloppy on the first night of murders. Manson sent out the original team again but added two additional members to go with them. Manson expected the race war to start after the first night of killings, and because it hadn't, he would be there to make sure it did start this time.

Leno, 44, and Rosemary, 36, LaBianca returned home to 3301 Waverly Drive around 2 a.m. after a weekend trip to a popular boating and camping spot about 150 miles from Los Angeles. They were both exhausted from their long journey and just wanted to change into their nightclothes, relax with some television, and go to bed.

Manson and his followers were out on the prowl all night looking for just the right people to attack but weren't having much luck. Manson remembered he had been to an LSD party one night on Waverly Drive, and kind of knew the neighborhood a little, so they headed there. When they got to the house where he had partied before, the place looked empty. Manson and his followers walked around the house, checking the doors and looking into any windows they could, only to find nothing was left in the house.

Then he heard a door slam, but it was coming from the next-door neighbor's house. He told the others to stay back, and he crept over towards the LaBianca house to check it out. Slowly and quietly, he looked into some of the windows and spotted Leno sleeping on his couch in the living room.

Manson went back and ordered his crew to follow him, and that he had found the one. They found a back door open and quietly crept into the house, going to the living room where Leno was. They bound his hands behind his back at gunpoint. They entered the bedroom where Rosemary was. There was a small struggle, but she was tied up and thrown on the bed. Then they moved Leno into the bedroom and put him on the bed with her.

The crew robbed whatever valuables and money they could get. Manson gave them instructions on how to kill the couple, and then he left. Tex Watson and Leslie van Houton both entered the bedroom, with Watson grabbing Leno and Van Houton holding Rosemary. Watson first stabbed Rosemary once and then handed the knife over to

Van Houton, who continued stabbing Rosemary at least 14 more times.

Later in court in 1971, Van Houton testified,

> "We started stabbing and cutting up the lady. I knew people would die. I knew there would be killing. I stabbed Mrs. LaBianca in the lower back 16 times because Manson wanted everyone to participate."

The bodies were discovered the next day by family members. Rosemary was stabbed in the back and buttocks, and there was a knife slash on her jaw. Leno was stabbed 36 times in the front of his body, and the Manson crew carved "War" onto his stomach and stuck him with a two-pronged carving fork. Both of the LaBiancas had pillowcases placed over their heads, and Rosemary also had a lamp cord wrapped around her neck.

There were bloody messages written around the house: "Rise," "Death to Pigs," and the misspelled "Healter (sic) Skelter" on the fridge door. This was the first clue that tied the two murders together.

Watson would later testify in court that Manson told him to,

> "kill everybody in the house as gruesome as I could."

FAMILY IN PRISON

It took a while for the police to catch the murderers. Over the years, there were many motives as to why this happened floating around in newspapers, books, and even movies. Some suggested police incompetence and that they lacked experience in such types of murders. Considering the time in which the crime happened, the late 1960s and early 1970s, police detachments were not connected by a national database. Each detachment ran their own investigations and rarely collaborated with other detachments. Even though the similarities in these two cases were apparent, without the two police detachments talking and exchanging information, they wouldn't see the connection. Remember, there was no internet at the time either, so communication between law enforcement agencies was slow at best.

Initially, Manson and 27 of his followers were arrested on Spahn Ranch for auto theft charges. Tex Watson and Patricia Krenwinkel left California right after the murders, so they were not arrested that day. While detained in jail, one of the Manson girls, Susan Atkins, started bragging to the other inmates about the murders she was involved in.

Eventually, her cellmates believed her and told the police about the things they heard from Atkins. Prosecutors approached Atkins in jail and offered her an immunity deal in exchange for her testimony against Manson and the others involved in the murders. She testified before a Grand Jury in December of 1969, and the trial against Manson and the others was set for three months later.

Before the trial was set to start, Atkins visited Manson in jail, and afterward, she told the State Attorney that she made the whole story up. The trial started in June 1970, with Manson, Atkins, Van Houten, and Krenwinkel facing murder charges for the Tate and LaBianca murders. Tex Watson was finally arrested in Texas but was fighting extradition, so he was tried separately in 1971.

The publicity surrounding the trial was like nothing that had ever been seen before. To keep the jury impartial, the Superior Court's Charles H. Older instituted a gag order that blocked all access to trial transcripts and forbade lawyers and witnesses from talking to the press about matters other than evidence entered in open court.

That wasn't easy, as Manson and his family kept it very entertaining. They often had some sort of display that shocked not only the country but the whole world. On the first day of trial, Manson, instead of appearing in a nice suit and clean-shaven, showed up in old baggy clothing and an "X" carved into his forehead, between his eyes.

After that, Atkins, Krenwinkel, and Van Houten copied him by shaving their heads and carving an "X" in each of their foreheads too. Later, according to Van Houten, they had been ordered by Manson to do it. Manson wanted to keep the court in a constant state of disruption, having his family members shout out and stage scenes during the trial. The court eventually banished them from the trial, and they moved to the streets outside of the courthouse and disrupted the street and road traffic around it.

Once during the trial, the Judge ruled against Manson while cross-examining a witness. Manson was so angry, he jumped out of his seat in court and onto the judge's bench holding a sharpened pencil towards his neck, screaming,

"In the name of Christian justice, someone should chop off your head!"

The court officers tackled Manson and removed him from the court. The judge was so scared after that attack by Manson, he started carrying a loaded .38 caliber gun to trial and kept it on his bench.

In August of 1970, President Nixon attended the Federal Law Enforcement Assistance Administration meeting in Denver, Colorado. The crime rate in the country had been steadily rising through the 1960s, and in fact, 1970 saw the highest increase of all time. At this meeting, Nixon gave a speech complaining about the media glorifying and making heroes out of criminals. Nixon then shockingly stated, "Manson was guilty, directly or indirectly, of eight murders without reason." This caused a firestorm in the media, as Nixon had inadvertently convicted Manson in the court of public opinion.

Nixon followed up with a speech at Andrews Airforce Base, claiming that what he meant to say was Manson was "charged" but not yet "guilty" of the eight murders. However, it was too late; the damage was done. The front pages of every newspaper screamed, "Manson Guilty, Nixon Declares." One of Manson's lawyers got a copy of the Los Angeles Times, that had such a headline, and gave it to him. During a day in the trial, Manson stood up and held the papers front page towards the jury. Manson's attorney then asked the judge to declare a mistrial as the jury was now tainted. After a long recess, the judge returned and allowed the trial to continue. He also gave

Manson's attorney a contempt of court charge, which resulted in one day in jail.

The state's main witness was Linda Kasabian, who was the driver in both attacks by the Manson family. She never asked for any immunity from prosecution. She was on the witness stand for 17 and a half days. Despite the incredible pressure she faced by the court proceedings, and from the long hard glares of Manson each day, she never broke down once.

Kasabian's testimony was the essential piece of the prosecution's case, as Manson didn't physically take part in any of the murders for which he was being tried. It was entirely a circumstantial conspiracy case. The prosecutor, Vincent Bugliosi, said, "I doubt we would have convicted Manson without her."

The state rested its case after four months of mainly witness testimony. Manson gave a nearly one hour speech to the court, with the jury absent. He claimed he was completely innocent, and that his girls, Van Houten, Atkins, and Krenwinkel, were all willing to testify that he was innocent.

The defense decided not to have any witnesses take the stand, including the Manson girls since their testimony would have incriminated them in the crimes. The girls asked their defense team to resign, as they no longer wanted to be represented by them. Just before the break when the court had ruled that the defense attorneys would all stay on the case, Manson stared over to Ronald Hughes, Leslie van Houten's attorney with great intensity, and said,

> "I don't ever want to see you in this courtroom again!"

After the Thanksgiving holiday recess, when the trial resumed, defense attorney Ronald Hughes, never returned to court. The police searched for four months, and on March 29, 1971, they found Hughes' dead body in a creek that runs through Ventura County. This happened to be the same day that the jury returned death penalty verdicts against all of the defendants in the Tate and LaBianca murders.

In his book, *Helter Skelter*, Vincent Bugliosi, wrote that Lynette 'Squeaky' Fromme, claimed that the Manson family killed more people and that Hughes was the first of the retaliation murders. But author and musician Ed Sanders, a close friend of Hughes, wrote a book called *The Family in 1971*, and he thought Hughes' death was accidental.

On January 25, 1971, Manson, Atkins, Krenwinkel, and Van Houten were found guilty of murder, and on March 29, 1971, they were each sentenced to death. Their time on death row was a short one, as the Supreme Court of California banned capital punishment in February 1972, and all the Manson Family sentences were commuted to life in prison.

In the subsequent years, Manson was convicted of two additional murders, Gary Hinman, a musician; and Donald Shea, a Spahn Ranch hand. There have been several rumors of the Manson family killing at least 35 more people that they buried in the desert, but Bugliosi didn't believe the number was near that high.

AND NOW, WHAT DO WE HAVE?

Nobody involved in the Tate and LaBianca murders has ever been released from prison.

Susan Atkins

Atkins died from brain cancer in 2009 at the Central California Women's Facility in Chowchilla. She became a born-again Christian shortly after her death sentence and was considered a model inmate. In 2008, Atkins applied for a compassionate release due to her terminal disease, but was opposed by Sharon Tate's sister, Debra, and Jay Sebring's nephew. The court denied her application.

Early Life

Born in San Gabriel, California, the second of three children, Susan Atkins grew up in northern California. According to Susan, her parents, Jeanette and Edward John Atkins, were alcoholics. Her mother died of cancer in 1963. Over the next three years, Susan's life was disrupted by the gradual breakup of her family, frequent relocations, and leaving home to live independently. Until she was 13 years old, Atkins and her family lived in a middle class home in the Cambrian Park area of San Jose, California.

She was described by those who knew her as a quiet, self-conscious girl who belonged to her school's glee club and the local church choir. Two weeks before her mother was hospitalized for the final time, Susan arranged for members of the church choir to sing Christmas carols under her bedroom window. After Jeanette Atkins' death, relatives were asked to help look after Susan and her two brothers.

Edward Atkins eventually moved to Los Banos, California, with Susan and her younger brother Steven. When he found work on the San Luis Dam construction project, Edward left the two children behind to fend for themselves. Susan took a job during her junior year in school to support herself and Steven. Atkins had been an average student in Leigh High School in San Jose, but her grades deteriorated when she entered Los Banos High School. During this time, she lived with various relatives.

Recruitment

In 1967, Atkins met Manson when he played guitar at the house where she was living with several friends. When the house was raided several weeks later by the police and Atkins was left homeless, Manson invited her to join his group. They were embarking on a summer road trip in a converted school bus painted completely black. She was nicknamed "Sadie Mae Glutz" by Manson and a man who was creating a fake ID for her at the time.

Atkins later claimed to have believed Manson was Jesus. At the Spahn Ranch in the San Fernando Valley in southern California, on October 7, 1968, Atkins bore a son by Bruce White, whom Manson called Zezozose Zadfrack Glutz. Atkins' parental rights were terminated once she was convicted of the murders, and no one in her family would assume responsibility for the child. Her son was adopted and renamed from the time of her incarceration in 1969. She had no further contact with him.

Murder One

During the summer of 1969, Manson and his commune at Spahn's Ranch were attracting the attention of the police, who suspected them of auto thefts and were suspicious of the high number of underage runaways. In an attempt to raise money to move away to the desert, Manson encouraged drug dealing. Purportedly, a botched drug scam by family member Tex Watson led Manson to confront and shoot a man by the name of Bernard "Lotsapoppa" Crowe. Manson believed he had killed Crowe, and he further believed Crowe was a Black Panther. Neither was true. Nonetheless, Manson feared retaliation from the Black Panthers and pressured his followers for more money. During this time, someone mentioned that an old friend, Gary Hinman, had just inherited a large sum of money. Manson hoped Hinman could be persuaded to join the commune and contribute his new inheritance.

Manson sent Atkins, Bobby Beausoleil, and Mary Brunner to Hinman's home on July 25, 1969. When she pleaded guilty to murder, Atkins claimed she didn't know a crime was going to take place, although she wrote in her 1977 book that she went to Hinman's home to get money and knew that they might have been going to kill him.

When Hinman insisted he had not inherited any money, Beausoleil beat him severely. When this didn't change Hinman's story, Manson showed up in person, and swung at his head with a sword, slicing his face and severely cutting his ear. Manson directed Atkins and Brunner to stay behind and tend to

Hinman's wounds. Two days later, and after a phone call from Manson, Beausoleil had Hinman sign over the registrations to his cars and then fatally stabbed him twice.

Beausoleil left a bloody handprint on the wall along with vague revolutionary words reportedly placed there in hopes of implicating the Black Panthers. Beausoleil was arrested on August 7, 1969, when he was found asleep in one of Hinman's vehicles. He was still wearing the blood-stained clothing he wore during the crime. The murder weapon was hidden in the tire well of the car's trunk.

Patricia Krenwinkel, now 72-years-old

Early life

Patricia Krenwinkel was born in Los Angeles, California, to an insurance salesman father and a homemaker mother. She attended University High School and then Westchester High School, both in the Los Angeles area. Patricia was often bullied at school by other students, suffered from low self-esteem, and was frequently teased for being overweight and for excessive growth of body hair caused by an endocrine condition.

After her parents divorced, 17-year-old Krenwinkel remained in Los Angeles with her father until she graduated from Westchester High School.

For a time, she taught Catechism (Roman Catholic religious instruction) and considered becoming a nun. She decided to attend the Jesuit college, Spring Hill College, in Mobile, Alabama. Within one semester, however, Patricia dropped out and moved back to California. Moving into her halfsister's apartment in Manhattan Beach, she found an office job as a processing clerk.

Recruitment

She met Charles Manson in Manhattan Beach in 1967, along with Lynette Fromme and Mary Brunner. In later interviews, Krenwinkel stated that she had slept with Manson the first night they met and that he was the first person who told her she was beautiful. Mesmerized by Manson's charisma and starved for attention, she decided to go to San Francisco with him and the other two girls, leaving behind her apartment, car, and last paycheck.

As the Manson Family grew, Katie (as Krenwinkel was now known) and the others went on a drug and sex filled 18-month tour of the American west in an old school bus. She would later recount an idealized version of The Family's early days:

> "We were just like wood nymphs and wood creatures. We would run through the woods with flowers in our hair, and Charles would have a small flute."

In the summer of 1968, Krenwinkel and fellow Family member, Ella Bailey, were hitchhiking around Los Angeles when Beach Boys founding member and drummer, Dennis Wilson, picked them up. After receiving an invitation to his home while he continued on to a recording session, Krenwinkel and Bailey were able to contact the Family and tell them of their new 'crash pad.' When Wilson returned later that evening, he found Manson and the rest of the Family eating his food, sleeping in his bedrooms, and partying inside and outside his home. After causing Wilson some financial problems, Manson and the rest of the Family left his mansion.

The hippie movement started to wind down in 1969, so Krenwinkel and the Family decided to live in isolation from the rest of society on Spahn's Ranch in the hills above the San Fernando Valley. Krenwinkel acted as a mother figure to the Family's several children and was seen as one of Manson's most intense and devoted followers.

Parole and Prison

Krenwinkel remained loyal to Manson for many years but eventually broke away from him. She maintained a perfect prison record and received a bachelor's degree in Human Services from the University of La Verne. She used her schooling in prison programs like Alcoholics Anonymous and Narcotics Anonymous. Krenwinkel first applied for parole on July 17, 1978, but was denied. She has since been to thirteen other parole hearings that have all ended in the same result. It seemed the question she always got wrong was when the parole board asked her who it was she thought she hurt the most. Krenwinkel always responded by telling them 'herself.' The parole board denied her saying that they felt Krenwinkel still posed an unacceptable risk to public safety.

Diane Sawyer interviewed Krenwinkel in 1994, and Krenwinkel said,

---

> "I wake up every day knowing that I'm a destroyer of the most precious thing, which is life, and I do that because that's what I deserve, is to wake up every morning knowing that."

In that same interview, she said that Manson was absolutely lying about not ordering the murders. Krenwinkel stated,

---

> "There wasn't one thing done that was even allowed to be done, without his express permission."

In Krenwinkel's parole hearing on December 29, 2016, her lawyers claimed that Krenwinkel was still suffering from "Battered Woman Syndrome" at the hands of Manson, during the times of the murders. The proceeding had to be postponed in order for a complete investigation to be done. Sharon Tate's sister, Debra, said,

---

> "Krenwinkel totally minimizes her actions and blamed everything on other people the whole trial."

This falls in line with how Krenwinkel responded to the parole board about her being the person hurt most by her actions.

Krenwinkel remains incarcerated in the California Institute for Women in Corona, California. She will be up for parole next in 2022.

Leslie Van Houten, now 70-years-old

Recruitment

After a few months in a commune in Northern California, Van Houten met Catherine Share and Bobby Beausoleil and moved in with them and another woman during the summer of 1968. The four broke up after jealous arguments, and Share left to join Charles Manson's commune. Van Houten, then aged 19, followed Share.

At this time, she phoned her mother to say she was 'dropping out' and would not be making contact again.

According to Van Houten, Manson controlled everything, deciding when they would eat, sleep, and have sex, and with whom they would have sex. He also controlled the use of LSD, giving followers larger doses than he took. According to Manson,

> "When you take LSD enough times, you reach a state of nothing, of no thought."

Van Houten stated she became 'saturated in acid' and could not grasp the existence of those living a non-psychedelic reality.

Re-trial

Van Houten was granted a retrial in 1977 due to the failure to declare a mistrial when her lawyer died. Her defense argued that Van Houten's capacity for rational thought was diminished due to LSD use and Manson's influence. The jury could not agree on a verdict. According to what the jury foreman later told reporters, they thought it was difficult, on the basis of the evidence, to determine whether Van Houten's judgment had been impaired enough for a verdict of manslaughter rather than first-degree murder.

It was reported in the news that because of time already served, Van Houten could go free that year if she was convicted of manslaughter. By law, prosecutors are not allowed to mention the possibility of the defendant being released on parole when arguing for a murder rather than manslaughter conviction because it is considered highly prejudicial to the defendant.

Second re-trial

The prosecution in 1970–71 had emphasized that the motive had nothing to do with robbery because the killers ignored valuable pieces of property. At Van Houten's second re-trial, the prosecution, who was now being aided by a specialist in diminished responsibility, altered the charges by using the theft of food, clothing, and a small sum of money taken from the house to add a charge of robbery. Whereby the felony murder rule tended to undermine a defense of reduced capacity. She was on bond for six months before being found guilty of first-degree murder. Van Houten was given a life sentence that entailed eligibility for parole, for which the prosecutor said she would one day be suitable.

Parole

Van Houten, the youngest of the Manson women in prison, has received the most controversy with her parole applications. She earned her bachelor's and master's degree while behind bars and was recommended for release by the California Parole Board in her last three attempts 2016, 2017, and 2019. In the first 2 cases, California Governor Jerry Brown rejected the release and later wrote,

> "After five decades, Van Houten has not wholly accepted responsibility for her role in the violent and brutal deaths of Mr. and Mrs. LaBianca."

In June of 2019, Governor Gavin Newsom also overruled the parole board decision to release Houten. He wrote in his judgement,

"While I commend Ms. Van Houten for her efforts at rehabilitation and acknowledge her youth at the time of the crimes, I am concerned about her role in these killings and her potential for future violence. Ms. Van Houten was an eager participant in the killing of the LaBiancas and played a significant role."

Charles 'Tex' Watson

Charles Denton Watson Jr. was born on December 2, 1945, in Farmersville, Texas, but grew up in nearby Copeville. He was the youngest of three children who grew up attending Copeville Methodist Church. Watson did well in school, was an athlete, and even wrote and edited for the school newspaper. He then moved to Denton, Texas, to attend the University of North Texas and was a member of the Pi Kappa Alpha fraternity.

Recruitment

In January 1967, Watson began working for Braniff International Airport as a baggage handler. One of the benefits of working for Braniff was the ability to travel for free on the airlines. Tex was very attracted to the new hippie lifestyle happening in Los Angeles and wanted to check it out. He used his free airline tickets to travel there and visit some of his fraternity brothers who lived in Los Angeles.

It's crucial to read in Watson's own words how he met Manson and became part of the Family. The following is directly from Tex Watson's website:

> "It began one night when I was driving out Sunset Boulevard toward the beach, heading home to Malibu. By then, I'd sold my T-Bird and had an old 1935 Dodge pickup. Hitchhikers were pretty common on Sunset, and I pulled over to pick one up. When he told me his name was Dennis Wilson, it didn't mean anything to me, but when he said he was one of the Beach Boys, I was impressed. I remembered all those surfing songs banging out of my brother's room back in Copeville. I grinned to myself, wondering what he would think if he could see me now with Dennis Wilson taking a ride in my truck and explaining how he'd wrecked his Ferrari and his Rolls Royce so was having to use his thumb.
>
> When we got to his house in Pacific Palisades, he invited me in. Rolling up the long driveway to what had once been Will Rogers's mansion, I played with the idea of what it would be like to tell my brother about the time one of the Beach Boys had me in for coffee. When we went inside, it was all I could do to keep my mouth closed. I'd never been in a place like this before. It was a long way from a three bedroom frame house in Texas.
>
> The first thing I saw when we came into the

kitchen was a heavyset, bald-headed man with a big gray beard pouring down his chest, sitting at the table with a few girls. He introduced himself as Dean Moorehouse. Over the next few months, Dean and I would become friends, despite the fact he was twice my age. I was to find out that he'd once been a Methodist minister, that up in Ukiah, California. After the Family left San Francisco, he'd gone after Charlie, ready to kill him for seducing his daughter Ruth (the one the Family came to call "Ouisch"). Instead of killing him, though, he ended up worshiping Charlie as Christ, after Charlie turned him on to LSD. Since then, he'd given up whatever Christian beliefs he'd once held and became a kind of wandering guru, teaching a lot of people in the film and music industries that true "awareness" and real "religion" came through opening yourself up with acid.

When people became aware, according to Dean, they could be free to die to themselves, to die to their egos. Then they would understand that Charles Manson was the reincarnation of the Son of God. Finding out all this came later, though. That night in the kitchen, he was just a fat old man with a greasy beard, trying to look like a hippie.

Almost as soon as I came in, he said there was somebody I should meet in the living room. I followed him. There he was — surrounded by five or six girls — on the floor next to the huge coffee table with a guitar in his hands. He looked up, and the first thing I felt was a sort of gentleness, an embracing kind of acceptance and love.

"This is Charlie," Dean said. "Charlie Manson."

There was a large ashtray full of Lebanese hash sitting in the middle of the coffee table. Pretty soon, Charlie and Dean and Dennis and I were lounging back on the oversized sofas, smoking. Nobody said much. As we got stoned, Charlie started playing his music, softly, almost to himself.

Here I was, accepted in a world I'd never even dreamed about, mellow and at my ease. Charlie murmured in the background, something about love, finding love, letting yourself love. I suddenly realized that this was what I was looking for: love. Not that my parents and brother and sister hadn't loved me, but somehow, now, that didn't count. I wanted the kind of love they talked about in the songs — the kind of love that didn't ask you to be anything, didn't judge what you were, didn't set up any rules or regulations — the kind of love that just accepted you, let you be yourself, do your thing whatever it was — the kind of love I seemed to be feeling right now, sitting around this coffee table getting zonked on some of the best hash I'd ever had, with a rock star and a fat old hippie and the little guy with the guitar who just kept singing softly, smiling to himself. It occurred to me that all the love in the room was coming from him, from his music.

Suddenly the girls came out of the kitchen and started serving us sandwiches they'd made — organic, full of sprouts and avocado and cheese. It was as if we were kings, just because we were men, and nothing could make them happier than waiting on us, making us happy. We all lay back and listened to Charlie sing to us about love — making love to us and for us with his music. I'd never known such peace.

Late that night at my truck as I was leaving, Dennis smiled and told me to come by anytime, take a swim in the pool, whatever I wanted. I drove out to Malibu, knowing that whatever had been going wrong in my life would be okay now. I'd found what really mattered: love between people, love that made all the old ideas about love as romance, or love as your parents pushing at you, just fade away. Charlie Manson was the first person I'd met who really knew what love was all about."

The Arrest and Trial

After the murders, on October 2, 1969, Watson fled the Spahn Ranch and headed back to his native Texas to hide from the authorities. But by November 30, 1969, he was arrested in Texas for the TateLaBianca murders. The prosecution applied to have Watson extradited from Texas back to California to stand trial with the rest of the Manson family, but Watson and his lawyers fought it. It took another nine months for the authorities to get Watson back to California.

When Watson arrived in California, he stopped talking and eating. He lost 55 pounds and became catatonic. He was admitted to Atascadero State Hospital for a 90-day evaluation to determine if he was fit to stand trial. Watson stayed there until February 1971, before he was finally deemed fit to stand trial. By then, the others had already been tried, so Watson stood trial on his own.

His trial lasted about seven months and ended in a conviction of seven counts of first-degree murder and one count of conspiracy to commit murder. The jury only took one week to determine that Watson was sane and responsible for his crimes. On October 21, 1971, Watson was sentenced to death. But he, too, escaped execution after the Supreme Court invalidated all death sentences imposed in California before 1972.

Parole and Prison

Watson converted to Christianity in 1975. He published *Will You Die for Me*, his autobiography, as told by Chaplain Ray Hoekstra in 1978. Watson married Kristin Joan Svege in 1979, and through their conjugal visits, had four children (three boys and one girl). In 1996, their conjugal visits were no longer allowed, and the couple divorced in 2003 after Svege met another man. They remained friends. Watson went on to become an ordained minister in 1981 and received his bachelor's degree in Business Management.

In August 1982, a Southern California-based group, "Citizens for Truth," submitted a petition with some 80,000 signatures and several thousand letters opposing Watson's parole. The group received support from Doris Tate, the mother of victim Sharon Tate. The group was asking the California Board of Prison Terms to deny parole for Watson. In later years, the group, along with Doris Tate, and her daughters, Patricia and Debra, submitted petitions with more than two million signatures.

In 2012, Watson disputed a request to release recordings of conversations with his attorney. The recordings became part of a bankruptcy proceeding involving the deceased attorney's law firm. Members of the Los Angeles Police Department (LAPD) said they believed the recordings might contain clues about unsolved murder cases involving the Manson family. Watson asked the presiding judge to allow police to listen to the tapes but not take possession of them. The LAPD did acquire the tapes, which allegedly contained Watson confessing to other murders but reported that they did not contain any new information. In September 2014, Richard Pfeiffer, an attorney for Leslie Van Houten, said that he was considering subpoenaing the tapes to look for information that might help Van Houten in her next parole hearing.

Today, Tex Watson is reportedly still an ordained minister and model prisoner who hasn't had any disciplinary issues since the 1970s. His ministry is called "Abounding Love," which has a website that's open to the public, though Watson does not have direct interactions with the website. Watson spends his days in prison, where he walks the tracks and eats only vegetarian, which keeps him healthy. Everywhere Watson goes or is seen, he is either singing Christian music or sharing his faith with others. On Watson's ministry website, he blogs about his life:

> "But I take full responsibility for my ignorance, lack of identity emptiness, and choice of life, which left me prey to his (Manson) deceptive plan. My actions were my own."

Watson's own minimum eligible parole date was November 26, 1976. He has been denied parole 17 times since then, including two stipulations. He was most recently given a five-year denial of parole at a board hearing on October 27, 2016.

He remains incarcerated at Richard J. Donovan Correctional Facility in San Diego, California.

Charles Manson

Manson was far less an ideal prisoner than his codefendants. During his time behind bars, we bore witness to the "X" that he carved into his forehead become a swastika; his receiving second and third-degree burns on nearly 20 percent of his body, mainly his face, hands, and scalp after he was doused with paint thinner by a fellow inmate, Jan Holmstrom in 1984 after Manson made fun of Holmstrom's religious belief of Hare Krishna; many escape attempts; his receiving more than 100 disciplinary infractions for things such as throwing coffee at a guards face, flooding out his cellblock, setting his mattress on fire, possessing a firearm, cell phone (several times), and drugs; and more.

Manson also filed for a marriage license in 2014, with his 27-year-old fiancé, Afton Elaine Burton, but they never went through with the marriage. Manson grew to be somewhat of a cultural icon to the newer generations who seemed to be interested in his status as a famous killer. In the 1980s, we saw the first sign of this when a group of satanic worshippers protested outside of San Quentin, insisting on Manson's release.

Thousands of t-shirts, sweaters, baseball caps, buttons, coffee cups, and other promotional merchandise with the likeness of Manson of them, were being sold and worn by people for decades.

Before his death in 2015, Vincent Bugliosi, author of *Helter Skelter*, gave the *Los Angeles Times* an interview, and one particular statement he made in that interview stuck with me:

> "Maniacs who kill to satisfy their urges do not resonate. Manson was different. As misguided as the murders were, he claimed that they were political and revolutionary, that he was trying to change the social order, not merely satisfy a homicidal urge. That appeals to the crazies on the fringes of society."

Manson's last parole hearing was on April 12, 2012. It was his 12th hearing, and it was denied just the same as the prior 11. Manson didn't physically appear at the hearing. He hadn't gone to them since his last appearance on March 27, 1997. At that last hearing, the parole board noted in their decision that Manson had a controlling behavior, mental health issues including schizophrenia and paranoid delusional disorder and was too great of a danger to be released.

The panel also noted several other things about

Manson - the 108 rule violations Manson acquired while in prison, the fact that he showed no sign of remorse, that he offered no insight to the panel as into the causative factors of the crimes, the fact that he lacked understanding of the magnitude of the crimes, that he was callous in his demeanor, and that Manson had no parole plans. They also decided at that hearing that Manson would not be reconsidered for another parole hearing for 15 years; so not before 2027, at which time he would be 92 years old if he was still alive.

Even after all the suffering this character Charles Manson caused to so many people, he still continues to make the headlines. Not only from the forums of news from his times but now with the new generation's social media trends. When Charles Manson recently died in 2017, there was no successor to decide what should be done with his body and possessions.

Four men made claims to Manson's remains. His body was placed on ice and remained there until the matter was settled in court. The California Superior Court awarded Manson's body to Jason Freeman, a 41-year-old oil rigger from Florida, who had found out earlier that year he was Manson's grandson.

Freeman did an article for *People* magazine discussing the fact that he was never able to meet his grandfather. What I found most shocking in his interview was when he stated,

---

> "He (Manson) would never kill a person carrying a baby."

Was this reference meant for the murder of actress Sharon Tate? It is well known that she was pregnant when she was murdered, and Manson was convicted of her killing.

Freeman held a cremation ceremony, not open to the public, in Porterville, California. There were 25 attendees at the service, including some former Family members. The mourners sang songs written by Manson, as well as songs by the Beach Boys and Guns N' Roses.

Spahn Ranch was once a place where Western movies were filmed, a tourist center, and now a daycare sits as an empty, overgrown property that's owned by the state.

The owner of the house that Sharon Tate and her friends were murdered in was owned by Rudolph Altobelli. It became a place where nobody wanted to live. *Life* magazine published an issue of their magazine with a photo of the grieving Roman Polanski sitting on the front porch of the Cielo Drive home. Altobelli pursued them in court, claiming the photo hurt the home's resale value. He eventually was able to get some tenants, the popular rock band, "Nine Inch Nails," but as soon as the band heard the sordid details about the house, they backed out of the lease. The house ended up being demolished in 1994 and was replaced with a massive Mediterranean style mansion. The new owner of the house, David Oman, claims the spirit of Sharon Tate haunts the house.

The LaBianca home is still standing on Waverly Drive, but the address has been changed.

The Early Years

Charles Manson was born on November 12, 1934, to

his 16-year-old mother, Kathleen Maddox. His father's name was never revealed, but his mother sued Colonel Walker Henderson Scott Sr. (1910-1954) of Catlettsburg, Kentucky, with a paternity suit that resulted in an agreed judgment in 1937. Scott wasn't a real Colonel, but just a nickname. He actually worked in local mills. When Maddox told him that she was pregnant with his baby, he responded by saying he was being called away for duty.

Before Manson's birth in August 1934, Maddox married William Eugene Manson (1909-1961), and he was listed on Charles' birth certificate. Manson's stepfather worked for a dry-cleaning business. His mother went on drinking benders for days at a time, leaving Charlie with her brother Luther, or anybody she could find to babysit. Manson's stepfather divorced Maddox within three years of their marriage on the charge of gross neglect.

On August 1, 1939, Maddox, her brother Luther, and Luther's girlfriend Julie Vickers decided they would rob a wealthy acquaintance of theirs. The three of them were caught within hours, arrested, and charged with robbery. All three of them were sent to jail, and Charlie was placed in foster care with his aunt and uncle in McMechen, West Virginia. Three years later, in 1942, Maddox was paroled, found her son Charlie, and they moved to Charleston, West Virginia.

A year later, Maddox married a man named Lewis, and she tried to get rid of Charlie. She sent him to the Gibault School for Boys in Terre Haute, Indiana, a school for male delinquents run by the Catholics. Charlie escaped from the school several times, but his mother always brought him back.

Many sordid stories have been told about Manson's

childhood. One report stated his mother sold him for a jug of beer to a woman, who was a stranger to Manson's mother, just because she wanted children. Manson's uncle had to search to find this woman, to bring Charles back home. But the key thing about his early years was the fact that it was marked with manipulated behaviors and mental illness.

His first arrest for theft happened in 1947, and he spent the next twenty years in and out of jail. In July 1961, Manson claimed his religion was 'Scientology,' and he identified as a Scientologist after studying the religion with a fellow inmate Lanier Rayner. Manson completed about 150 hours of auditing for the Church, before declaring Scientology was "too crazy" for him.

Following his last release from jail in 1967, Manson decided to head to California and become a musician with his new long-haired hippie look. Vincent Bugliosi wrote in a *Rolling Stone* article in 2013:

> "He had a quality about him that one-thousandth of one percent of people have. An aura. Wherever he went, kids gravitated toward him."

A lot of those kids were just drifting from place to place without any sort of purpose. They didn't have any faith in the direction their own parents had taken in their lives, so they were searching for something else. They wanted something with meaning, not just for money.

These vulnerable kids were perfect for Manson. He focused in on their weaknesses and brainwashed them to follow him, promising all the while that he would help them find their way. He used LSD, sex, bible readings, and rambling lectures about a revolution to brainwash them. He made them all listen to the same songs from the Beatle's White Album for hours at a time.

Basically, they were indoctrinated through a series of acid trips, mandatory orgies, and hypnotic repetitive lectures outlining the upcoming race war from the words of the songs on the Beatles' White Album.

Was Charlie's use of LSD during the growth of his family part of the mind control he needed?

By the time David Smith opened the medical clinic (HAFMC) on 558 Clayton Street, San Francisco, in June 1967, he had already been doing years of drug research and had sociological interests in studying with the new youth. At this clinic was where Manson developed his skills for gaining such a strong following of believers.

The clinic was an instant success, treating hundreds of patients a day, offering care for those suffering from overdoses, or bad trips, providing information about sexually transmitted diseases, providing food for the hungry, and counseling for those who needed it most. The clinic was staffed entirely with volunteers and was not authorized by any governmental association, which made it even more popular. It was decorated with wild psychedelic colors and peace signs all over the walls.

As mentioned previously, Charles Manson and his family became regulars at this clinic, with the girls being treated for sexually transmitted diseases and unwanted pregnancies. Manson rented an apartment a few blocks away from the clinic, so it was convenient for him to avail of their services. The Manson Family members were such frequent visitors to the clinic, the staff knew them as "Charlie's Girls," and noticed how they referred to Manson as "J.C." or "Christ" and served his every need.

According to Smith, the clinic is where Manson learned how to reprogram his followers, using a combination of LSD and mind games:

> "Manson would force his followers to submit to unconventional sexual practices. He would invoke mysticism and pop psychology as the acid took hold, saying, "You have to negate your ego." He was treating the girls like they were objects and eroded any independence that they had, turning them into computers or empty vessels that would accept almost anything he told them. It wasn't long before they started to obey Manson without question. The Acid was unmistakably essential in the process."

8

ROD FERRELL'S VAMPIRE CULT

"Going into the electric chair is, as morbid as it may sound, it's been a fantasy of mine." - Rod Ferrell

---

Not all doomsday cults have a leader who thinks that they are Christ and follow scriptures from the Abrahamic Gods. There are many religions that worship paranormal characters or are occult based. Paganism, with its witches and warlocks, includes the worshipping of nature and old pagan gods and goddesses. Modern-day occult groups quite often worship pop culture fictional characters that come to life through them. One such group was called "Rod Ferrell's Vampire Clan."

Rod Ferrell believed that he had been alive for over five centuries. He had grown tired of life but was cursed with immortality. In the 1990s, he came back to live in our modern society.

He also believed he last lived among humans in 1400 France, where he was a member of the wealthy upper class. But for the past 500 years, he had been a spirit. And even though he enjoyed being a spirit, he knew it was time to return to flesh. Only this time, he would live among the lower-class community of Murray, Kentucky, a college town of about 17,000 people that houses over 75 religious assemblies, with Baptist being the most popular.

Ferrell convinced his followers that he was a 500-year-old vampire named "Vesago," who was equal to a God. He felt it was appropriate that he chose America to live in, as they have committed so many sins, and threatened to destroy the planet. Ferrell insisted he was called upon by Lucifer to build up an army to stop a coming apocalypse.

SO HOW DID THIS HAPPEN?

Rod Ferrell was born on March 28, 1980, to two teenage parents, Rick and Sondra Ferrell. The couple was married about a week after Rod was born but separated within two weeks. Rick left to join the military and left Sondra and Rod with her parents. Rod was gang-raped by his grandfather and his grandfather's friends when he was five years old. But because of financial difficulties, they continued living with her father. When Rod was 16 years old, his mother remarried, moved to Michigan and left Rod behind in Murray.

Growing up, Rod was exposed to occult rituals, human sacrifices in games such as "Dungeons and Dragons," and the role-playing "Vampire: The Masquerade" game.

Around this time, Rod started failing in school, skipping classes, smoking on school grounds, and defying his teachers. Instead of doing his schoolwork, Rod spent his time going to cemeteries, where he cut himself and drank his blood.

His mother's marriage didn't work out, so she returned to Murray after she left her husband. But instead of dealing with Rod's apparent issues, she encouraged him to skip school, use drugs, and role-play all night long. Sondra took up with another boyfriend, Stephen Murray, who helped Rod increase his knowledge of vampires by teaching him real-life vampire role-playing scenarios.

In September 1996, during one of their real life role-playing games, Murphy ended up attacking Rod, sending him to the hospital. But Rod refused any treatment. Murphy was charged with assault and convicted. His mother, Sondra, was charged with soliciting a minor, Murphy's 14-year-old brother, when she sent him love letters asking to be his vampire bride.

During his mother's arrest and trial, Rod went to stay with his father, Rick, now living in Eustis, Florida. While he was there, he met 15-year-old Heather Wendorff, who lived with her parents, Rick and Naomi. Rod encouraged Heather to skip school to spend time with him instead. The relationship made her become aloof around her family and grow very close to Ferrell. He was able to communicate with her without words, but by just looking into her eyes.

Heather felt lust for Ferrell, and her thoughts became all about him. She was slowly being drawn into his world and his idea of spirituality.

Rod took Heather to the Greenwood Cemetery to teach her witchcraft and explain the importance of sacrifice. He convinced her that killing did not break nature's rules. He told Heather that he could smell her blood and that it was sweet, unlike the vile blood of vampires.

The only other friend Heather confided in was Jeanine, who she thought could help her figure out what was real and what was just Ferrell's fantasies. Rod told them that he believed Heather was a prophet, and Jeanine was an ancient queen, scaring them so much they broke into a shaky laugh. They both knew Ferrell said a lot of things that didn't make sense. They didn't believe it all, but none of that mattered. Both of them loved immersing themselves into his stories and found it much more interesting than the regular world in which they lived.

If either of the girls ever doubted anything Rod said, it was never displayed in front of him. Both Heather and Jeanine were infatuated with Ferrell. But it was Jeanine who felt that she was in love with him and became his girlfriend. They would never contradict him in public. However, they both thought that when Rod was his vampire alter ego, he reminded them of the character "Louis" from the movie *The Interview with the Vampire*.

One day Rod decided he would show Jeanine the ceremonial altar he had made in his bedroom at home. He invited her and her friend, Eric, over to hear him recite an incantation. During his recital, he grabbed a razor blade and sliced his forearm open. Rod turned to Jeanine and ordered her to drink his blood.

Assuming her friend Eric would protect her, she said no, but Eric was transfixed. He decided to drink the blood from Rod's arm himself. Rod then cut his fingertip with the razor and walked over to Jeanine and stuck his finger in her mouth. She was resistant at first, but he reassured her that he didn't have human blood. She then started to suck on his finger and drink his blood.

The bloodlettings became a regular occurrence after that, with each of the participants cutting themselves and drinking each other's blood. It was like watching a B-grade movie, with Anti-Christ Superstar playing, incense, and candles burning.

Heather became depressed and obsessed with death. Her parents tried to get her to join the Episcopalian Church in town. But Heather wanted nothing to do with any official religion or church. She no longer believed anything they stood for. In her opinion, all churches were superficial and just about money, not their patrons.

Heather wanted to leave her town badly, but she couldn't. So in her mind, she followed Ferrell from where she was. She had fantasies of seeing angels, demons, ghosts, and vampires every day in every place she would go. She desired to learn from every spirit she encountered. She thought that if she did, she could wield power to raise herself above the human race. She believed she was evolving into a high priestess.

Heather watched with amazement when Rod recited the Lord's Prayer backward, all while holding the Bible in one hand, and an upside-down cross in the other. The vision made her tingle throughout her body, almost electric, and she felt amazing and led to her uncontrollable laughter.

Ferrell explained to her how the realm of eternal was ruled by evil. He read from the book *Necronomicon* which was supposedly written by a 'Mad Arab.' Ferrell explained how the ancient ones, who came from a dead civilization, were the ones to guard the gates of hell. This book also taught incantations, exorcisms, and bindings, and held the secrets and power of the ancient ones. They would have to decipher the meanings hidden in the book in order to step up on the ladder of lights, to the gates of hell. One time, Rod and Heather performed a blood-bonding ritual from the book, where they mixed body fluids, which they believed resulted in Heather being another step closer to redemption. In reality, Ferrell purchased *Necronomicon*, in paperback, at Walden Bookstore.

Eventually, Heather started to believe Rod, indeed, was a vampire. He appeared to go through weird transformations that made him seem like he existed from the very beginning of time. She felt very connected with him, as she was so much like him. The more time Heather spent with him, the more she felt that pain and suffering would be her only way to freedom. She was at the point where she allowed Rod to drink blood directly from her body.

The time had come for Rod to move back to Murray, and he had to say goodbye to the group. He promised them that he would come back someday and that he would always love them. The four of them, Rod, Heather, Jeanine, and Eric, would have one last bloodletting ritual together at his house, and Rod left the next morning. Even with Rod gone, Heather kept believing in the lifestyle in which he had introduced her.

After Ferrell moved back to Murray, Kentucky, he became Heather's pen-pal. Over the next year, Heather told Ferrell that she needed help to run away from her home. She said living there was like living in "hell." It was reported that Heather told him she was being abused by her parents.

For Rod, after returning to Murray, the activities of the vampire group turned violent. They escalated to the point where they broke into an animal shelter and killed two dogs. One of the dogs Rod stomped to death and the other he pulled it's legs off.

The regular group of five teenagers in Ferrell's Vampire Clan consisted of Rod; Heather; Dana Cooper, 19; Charity Keesee, 16, of Murray; and Scott Anderson, 16, of Mayfield. There had been a few other members in the group, but because of the escalation in violent activities, they decided to leave.

On November 25, 1996, Richard Wendorf, 49, Heather's father, was sleeping on his sofa, while his live-in girlfriend, Naomi Ruth Queen was in the shower. Both Heather and her sister Jennifer were out for the evening. Ferrell and Scott Anderson entered their home through the unlocked garage. Ferrell beat Wendorf with a crowbar that he had picked up while coming through the garage, which broke his skull and ribs before killing him.

Naomi got out of the shower and went into the kitchen to get a cup of coffee. There she encountered Ferrell, who was covered in blood and held a crowbar. She screamed and grabbed the pot of coffee that she had made earlier and threw it at Farrell. He had initially meant for Naomi to live, but when she surprised Ferrell, he reacted by hitting her with the crowbar.

After the two were dead, Ferrell burned marks in the shape of a V's and dots onto the bodies. This represented that the deceased were now considered to be in the cult. Ferrell rifled through Wendorf's pockets and found the keys to his Explorer and a Discover credit card. The two drove off in the Explorer to meet with Keesee, Cooper, and Heather, who was driving a Buick. They drove to a nearby town, Sanford, and dumped the Buick after removing the license plates and putting them on the stolen Explorer.

The five of them drove on Interstate 10 through Tallahassee and towards New Orleans, intending to meet the famous vampire author Anne Rice. They were tracked to a town called Crestview when they used Wendorf's credit card to buy a knife and some gas. After four days on the road, the group made it to Baton Rouge and were caught shortly after. One of the girls, Charity Keesee, phoned her grandmother in South Dakota, to ask her if she could borrow some money. Keesee's grandmother informed the police that the group had been hiding out in the Howard Johnson hotel.

After the arrest, they were held in the Baton Rouge jail until they were extradited to Florida. The four group members were all charged with murder, but the daughter of the murdered couple, Heather, was not indicted.

Ferrell was charged with armed burglary, armed robbery, and two counts of first-degree murder. His trial began on February 12, 1998, and Ferrell pled guilty to the killings, claiming that the others traveling with him were innocent, except for Scott Anderson. It only took two weeks for the jury to convict both Ferrell and Scott of all four charges and sentence Ferrell to death, and Anderson to life in prison. For two years, Ferrell was the youngest person ever to be on death row, but later, the supreme court of Florida reduced his sentence to life without the chance of parole. Anderson was later resentenced to 40 years, and Ferrell is currently attempting the same. He is hoping the court will reduce his life sentence and consider his childhood trauma as a reason to reduce his sentence.

Ferrell's lawyer argued that his young age should be a mitigating factor in his sentence, as well as his emotional age, which was determined at age three. Furthermore, Ferrell was diagnosed with a schizotypal personality disorder, Asperger's syndrome, PTSD from the sexual assault when he was five years old and claimed to have seen angels and demons.

Charity Keesee was convicted of two counts of third-degree murder, robbery with a gun or deadly weapon, and burglary armed with weapons or explosives. She was sentenced to 10.5 years in state prison. Dana Cooper was also convicted of the same charges, but she was given a 17.5-year sentence. Heather was never charged but remains estranged from her family.

SO, DO VAMPIRES REALLY EXIST?

Vampirism within the paranormal subculture includes both sanguinarian vampirism, which involves blood consumption, and psychic vampirism, whose practitioners believe they are drawing spiritual nourishment from vibrations surrounding a living creature or vital life force energy.

There are several types of vampire lifestyles. Though many modern vampires are part of small clans, called covens or houses, there are also many that chose to live solitary lives as a vampire:

- **Sanguinarian vampires** - those who consume the blood of others as a form of energy-taking;
- **Psychic vampires** - sometimes called "psi vamps," vampires in this role claim to attain nourishment from the aura, psychic energy, or pranic energy of others. They believe one must feed on this energy to balance a spiritual or psychological energy deficiency, such as a damaged aura or chakra;
- **Hybrid vampires** - vampires who take both blood and psychic energy as a form of nourishment;
- **Blood donors** - people who willingly allow vampires to drink their blood. Within vampire society, vampires and donors are considered equal, though donors are expected to have some subservience to their vampires. Donors can prove difficult for those in the vampire lifestyle to find;
- **Blood fetishists** - members of the vampire community who use blood as a stimulant, or consider blood-drinking a sexual fetish, sometimes using or drinking it during sadomasochistic sex;
- **Vampire role-players** - sometimes referred to as "fashion vamps," these members of the vampire subculture differ in that they acknowledge being only fans of vampire subculture. They dress up in vampire clothing, live a vampire lifestyle (e.g., sleep in coffins), and primarily participate in roleplaying games such as *Vampire: The Masquerade*.

9

CHILDREN OF GOD (THE FAMILY INTERNATIONAL)

"We're even going to have sex in Heaven! How about that?" - David Berg

---

"The Family International" (TFI) is a Christian communal cult founded in Huntington Beach, California, in 1968. It was initially called the "Teens for Christ" and later changed to "The Children of God." In the

last few years, they have reorganized and are now known as the "Family of Love" or just "The Family." They have existed of several communes in cities all over the world.

The founder of the movement was David Berg, a former Christian and Missionary Alliance pastor. Berg communicated with his followers by writing and publishing letters, that he called "Mo Letters." He sent these letters over a 24-year period, until 1994 when he died. In one of his 1972 letters, he claimed to be the prophet of God and his end-time messenger. At the time of his death, there were 130 Children of God communes around the world following Berg's prophecies.

In 1978, the Children of God reorganized after reports of serious misconduct, including financial mismanagement and the use of what was called "Flirty Fishing."

Flirty Fishing was introduced as an evangelizing tool, that encouraged female members to show God's love through sexual relationships with potential converts to the group. This 'tool' was started by Berg in 1973, and at first, only included the members in his inner circle. But by 1976, Flirty Fishing became practice for the general membership. After the scandals became public, roughly one-eighth of their followers left the group, and those that remained became the Family of Love, and then later, The Family.

The group used escort agencies to meet potential members. According to The Family International, there were over 100,000 people who received God's gift of salvation through Jesus because of Flirty Fishing. Researcher, Bill Bainbridge, obtained data from The Family International, claiming that from 1974 to 1987, members had sexual contact with 223,989 people while using this method of conversion.

Karen Zerby, known to the group as Mama Maria, assumed leadership after Berg died. Under her leadership, the cult drafted a "Love Charter" that included strict fundamental family rules that defined the rights and responsibilities of each member.

In a 1995 British Court ruling, it was stated that the group had in the past engaged in abusive sexual practices involving minors and had also used severe corporal punishment and sequestration to minors. However, the court also ruled that those practices were part of the former group's behavior but had been abandoned by the new leadership. The ruling went on to say that it was now a safe environment for children. The Love Charter of the new group set the rules of the group and has been in place ever since.

The Family believes they are a spiritual army in a war of good versus evil for the souls and hearts of men. They have spiritual helpers, which include angels, departed humans, and religious or mythical figures from history. Some of their helpers are the goddess Aphrodite, Merlin, the Sphinx, Elvis, Marilyn Monroe, Audrey Hepburn, Richard Nixon, and Winston Churchill.

The members describe their relationship with Jesus to be a loving one, which includes intimacy and sex. They believe that the female members are all Christ's brides, and are called to love and serve him with 'wifely fervor.' They even go so far as to imagine Jesus is joining them during any sexual intercourse or masturbation.

The male members are told they should picture themselves as a woman to avoid a homosexual relationship with Jesus.

Much of the Family's publications have messages that are believed to be directly from Jesus. In them, it is believed he claims to need these intimate and sexual encounters. One such encounter was written in a book titled *Zealot* by Jo Thornely.

Berg taught his followers that God gave us flesh, so flesh should be exposed and celebrated. The female followers were encouraged to glorify God by dancing in videos that were sent to Berg. The leader requested the dancers start off dancing slowly, with a veil on, and gradually go faster, eventually removing the veil and fondling themselves. He required only women and young girls who were in good shape, not pregnant, do these videos. Basically, he had the group create porn for him in a collection of videos.

According to Jo Thornely, via a newsletter, Berg also suggested sexy things the women and girls could say in these videos while they were pretending to make love to Jesus. Berg did this to make sure that none of them ran out of ideas when they were 'talking dirty' to Jesus. Such as, "I receive your love, Lord, with open arms and open legs!" or "Flood me with your seeds!" and "My pussy is hungry for you, Jesus!"

Women were required to have sex with any of the men in the group, even if they didn't want to. It was considered their duty. Men had sex with anyone they wanted in their own homes. It got to the point where there was actually a "share schedule" created so they could be organized about their swinging sexual lifestyle.

Berg taught the group that exclusive twosomes were

selfish and should be abandoned for the greater good of the larger communal family. This was saying the women were created for men by God, and that was their main purpose. It was God's way of saying that he loved the men.

Famous people that have been members in this church include River Phoenix, Joaquin Phoenix, Rain Phoenix, Rose McGowan, who have all been famous actors.

Ricky Rodriguez was considered the prince of the cult. His mother, Karen Zerby, was married to the leader David Berg. He was fathered after she had 'flirty fished.' Rodriguez was always told that he would be the one to lead them through end times.

Rodriguez's upbringing was chronicled in *The Davidito Book* and was distributed among the cult members as a how-to-guide for raising children. The book included several pictures of Rodriguez with an array of nannies he had throughout his youth. The nannies were all topless.

In 1995, Rodriguez married Elixa Munumel, from Budapest, and the two of them left The Family in 2001. However, the pair were unable to keep their relationship a happy one, and they went separate ways in 2004. Rodriguez moved to Tucson, Arizona, and worked as an electrician. According to his friends, Rodriguez was obsessed with finding his mother, who was in hiding after he spoke out against her. He held terrible resentment toward his parents because of all the sexual abuse he encountered.

In January 2005, Rodriguez arranged a meeting with Angela Smith to go for dinner with him in Tucson. Smith was a member of the cult and one of his former nannies that had sexually abused him, and others, years before.

After their dinner, he brought her to his apartment, where he stabbed her to death. Afterward, he got in his car and drove across the California border, to a small town called Blythe. He parked his car and called his ex-wife from his cell phone. Rodriguez explained to her what he had done and why. He hung up the phone and shot himself in his head with a semi-automatic gun.

Rodriguez recorded a videotape the night before he killed Smith and committed suicide. The video, which was provided to *The New York Times* by Rodriguez's wife, was made in his apartment in Tucson and showed him loading a gun and showing off other weapons. He said he saw himself as a vigilante, avenging children like him and his sisters who had been subject to rapes and beatings:

> “There's this need that I have. It's not a want. It's a need for revenge. It's a need for justice because I can't go on like this."

Rodriguez was not the only suicide among people reared in the Children of God. Some former members who kept in touch with one another through a website, movingon.org, said that in the last 13 years, at least 25 young people reared in the cult had committed suicide.

The Family International today

Rodriguez’s suicide brought the cult back into the public eye. Child abuse accusations in the cult arose in Argentina, Australia, France, and Spain. Some members were jailed, but none of the top leaders of the cult were convicted of anything.

Rodriguez's mother, Karen Zerby, still leads the cult. But her location and travel schedules are kept secret from not only the public but most cult members.

There are an estimated 10,000 members who live in more than 700 communal households in about 100 countries, according to The Family International, making it the most successful communal group that originated in the counterculture era.

TFI describes itself as a Christian fellowship dedicated to sharing God's word and love with others. Their mission statement is:

> "to comfort, aid, and minister to those in need, endeavoring to follow the example of Jesus."

The Love Charter is still The Family's governing document that encompasses each member's rights, responsibilities, and requirements. Other governance documents exist for certain members - the Missionary Member Statutes, and Fellow Member Statutes.

Homes are reviewed every six months against a published set of criteria in The Love Charter to ensure compliance.

TFI believes that the following Biblical passage refers to an increasing amount of spiritual authority given to Peter and the early disciples.

> "I will give you the keys of the kingdom of heaven, and whatsoever you bind on earth will be bound in heaven, and whatsoever you loose on earth will be loosed in heaven," (Matthew 16:19)

It also believes this passage refers to keys that were hidden and unused in the centuries that followed but were again revealed through Karen Zerby.

TFI members call on the various "Keys of the Kingdom" for extra effect during prayer. The Keys, like most TFI beliefs, were published in magazines that looked like comic-books to make them teachable to children. These beliefs are still generally held and practiced today.

10

THE ANT HILL KIDS

"The commune lives on. It's an indication of the power of the man—those women are there for him. Who knows whether he has reformed?" - Maclean's

Roch Theriault had a long black beard, sharp blue eyes, and always dressed in basic clothes. He had the look of a prophet, like Moses, that you would see on an old movie from the 1960s. So much so that members of his cult called him just that, Moses.

Only Theriault had many differences from Moses. He was an alcoholic, had eight wives, and punished his followers by pulling out their teeth, severing their arms or legs, and even disembowelment. He had a small group of followers, including eight women, two men, and 28 children; he was the father of most of the children. Theriault named his followers the "Ant Hill Kids," and he convinced them all that he was taking them to the promised land.

Like many other cults that have come before, Theriault started luring followers into his group on the premise of learning how to live healthier and better lives. In 1979, the cult lived outside in the Canadian outdoors so they could stay on track with living a clean, healthy life. But it quickly turned into more of a prison, where nobody could leave.

Followers were reliant on Theriault to supply their basic needs, such as food and water, and he had brainwashed them with dramatic sermons warning them that the end of the world was near.

Over the years, each doomsday time Theriault set came and went, with no end occurring. But still, the followers remained. He was brutal to anyone in the group that challenged him, especially the men.

The cult remained together until 1989 when one of the wives escaped in the woods, missing her right arm. Several of the children and other wives were later found dead when the authorities arrived at the camp.

BACKGROUND

Roch Theriault was born on May 16, 1947, in Thetford Mines, Quebec, a small mining town about 65 miles from

Quebec City. He attended a four-room school until he reached grade 7. Along with his family, he belonged to the Pilgrims of St. Michael, which was a Roman Catholic movement. They were an easily-spotted religious group that wore white berets, not only in church, and while they went door to door spreading the word, but in their everyday life as well.

The Pilgrims promoted having an equitable class structure and disbanding the national banks. It was during these days when Theriault developed a deep hatred for the Catholic Church. In the early part of the 1970s, Theriault was bankrupt, had no job, but a wife and two children to support. He immersed himself in religion and medicine by reading everything that he could find in bookstores and the library. He eventually left the Pilgrims and joined the Seventh Day Adventist church.

Considered to be a protestant denomination with apocalyptic beliefs, the Seventh-day Adventists encouraged a vegetarian diet and clean living long before it was commonplace in western society. Before long, Theriault was teaching a class on how to quit smoking and was very popular with the congregation of his new church. But like most religions, there was a hierarchy, and the leadership felt challenged by his newfound popularity and thought he was too arrogant. So, he was thrown out of the church. When Theriault left, he took some followers with him.

One of those who left with Theriault was Gabrielle Lavallee. She was working as a nurse but had issues. She didn't find the help to change her life with the SDA and liked Theriault, so she left with him.

> "I was wondering who I really was. I wondered what I was doing on Earth. I was wondering where I was coming from. I didn't have very much confidence in myself. I didn't believe in myself."

But after joining Theriault's cult, she became a stripper and started using drugs regularly.

According to the book *Savage Messiah* written by Paul Kaihla and Ross Lavar, things started to make sense to Gabrielle as soon as she met Theriault. She felt comfortable with him and was able to tell him her story. She wasn't proud of the things she had done, but her dreams and daytime visions seemed to indicate that higher power and purpose in her life was yet to be discovered. In one of those dreams, she saw a man in her room who resembled Theriault. She took that as a sign he was meant to be in her life, and they were meant to be together.

At the same time, Theriault was preaching to people in the church that he was speaking directly to God. And because of that, he was starting a natural healing center. He asked Lavallee to join his new clinic, which was a once in a lifetime opportunity for her. Lavallee excitedly agreed, unaware that this would be the beginning of a very long 11 years of her life with a maniac.

Once the natural healing center was up and running, Theriault offered alternative treatments to its patients. One 'treatment' included a prescription for grape juice to one of his leukemia patients. The woman soon died afterward.

By the summer of 1978, Theriault started moving his cult in a different direction. He decided it was no longer his job to help people with their minor needs, such as health or eating correctly. He had now been given a more critical task. God had warned him that the end of the world was fast approaching, and even provided Theriault with the date of February 17, 1978, as the end of time.

Theriault believed that he and his group could only survive if they took refuge in the forest. The group moved to the bush and waited for the end. They were God's chosen ones that would rebuild the world out of the destruction left behind by the nonbelievers. So Theriault and his group of nine women, four men, and a few children set off to the eastern Quebec forests to prepare for the end times and the work that would come afterward in rebuilding.

PROMISED LAND

In July, Theriault and his group found what he considered the perfect location for their task in the thick Canadian woods of the Gaspe Peninsula. They lived in tents while they built their communal log cabin, designed by Theriault, and, of course, by the word of God. His followers were up by 5 a.m. every morning and worked until dark. They ate, received a sermon from Theriault, went to sleep, just to repeat the same process the next day, and every other day after that for as long as it would take to get the project done before the harsh Canadian winter set in.

As each night passed, Theriault's sermons became more like lectures and demands of his followers. He preached about the corrupt nature of society and the evil within conventional families. The children were made to speak about how their parents never gave them anything good, and the only person to have ever given them anything good was Theriault.

The group completed the cabin in August, just in time to beat the winter. Theriault was now able to christen each of his members with biblical names. Theriault's wife would be known "Esther," a queen who saved the Jews from mass slaughter in ancient Persia.

Theriault changed his name to "Moses," after the Old Testament hero, who led God's people out of the darkness and into the promise of a bright everlasting life.

As the Ant Kids group began to settle into their new rural setting home, they noticed that Theriault was no longer eating the holistic clean living diet he had preached about in hundreds of his sermons.

Instead, he was eating meat, drinking soda pop, and even munched on potato chips. Unknown to the group, Theriault was pimping out one of his girls as payment for these provisions that came from a local store.

In September, Theriault's wife, Esther, was now about six months pregnant and unable to have sex again until the baby was delivered. So, he started selecting other female followers to become his spiritual wives. Theriault cited Biblical stories of men who had several wives. Such as, King David, the second King of Israel, and Judah, who was married to at least seven women and also had concubines.

Theriault's harem didn't end after Esther had her baby. Instead, it grew even larger.

Eventually, Theriault started having polygamist marriage ceremonies, with most of the wives not in attendance. Theriault also caused fights between his wives, by making them do things to gain his attention and vie for his joining them in their bed for the night. It is estimated that Theriault fathered 28 children in this cult.

After the end times date, February 17, 1978, came and went without the apocalypse, Theriault attributed the mistake to God having a different clock than humans. At this point, his followers fit into either of two categories:

1. A total believer that Theriault was the speaker for God, having unconditional support for him, or
2. A skeptic of Theriault that wavered in their support or belief, but were too scared of him after years of being beaten, humiliated, attacked during his drunken rages, and isolated from the rest of the world to leave.

Theriault's method of abusing and humiliating a member in front of the whole group was so intense no one would ever dare to try and stop it. They were terrified of Theriault moving his assault towards them instead.

Another two years passed before Theriault, and his group captured the attention of law enforcement. Whenever Theriault or any members had to leave the camp or were given work away from their children, Theriault assigned one member, Guy Veer, to be responsible for all the children. Guy Veer was a former patient in a mental hospital being treated for depression.

On March 23, 1981, Jacques Giguere and his wife Maryse Grenier, were sent to do some work for Theriault. They left their 2-year-old son Samuel with Veer.

Often, while the children played, Veer just slept through the day. He only woke if there was a fight or someone screamed. On this particular day, Samuel kept crying every time Veer was trying to get to sleep. Each time the child would wake him up, Veer responded by punching the child in the face until he went quiet. Later that evening, the group's nurse Gabrielle Lavallee, examined the child and decided it would be best to keep him in her care.

Over the next few days, the boy was unable to sit up on his own or eat any solid food. Lavallee also located an egg-sized swelling on the boy's penis, which prevented him from being able to urinate. It was discovered later that they had tried to circumcise the toddler themselves without using alcohol to clean the wound.

When Theriault heard about the boy's condition, he decided he would have to perform surgery on the boy. Theriault made an incision in the boy's penis, using a pair of scissors. The lump drained, and he applied a paste that Lavallee had made from iodine, olive oil, and plantain. The next day the child became so sick that he could only be fed fluids from a dropper. The child died the following day. Theriault decided to burn the toddler's body 'so that no wild animals could consume his corpse.'

Time passed without mention of the boy's death. Theriault later castrated Veer for an unknown reason. It was suggested that he had attempted to assault some of the other members in the camp sexually, but there is no direct evidence of this. After he was castrated, Veer escaped from the group and moved to a nearby town. There, he told his neighbor some of the details of the cult, including about the dead boy.

The story got back to the police, who raided the commune. The police arrested Theriault, and the dead boy's parents. Veer himself was also arrested a few days after that. Ultimately, Theriault, the boy's parents, and Veer were found guilty of the death of the child, Samuel Giguere.

Theriault only served two years in prison for the crime, and during that time, he kept in constant contact with the remaining members of his cult. He promised them that the group would live together again, peacefully, and happily move forward.

When he was released, he reassembled the Ant Hill Kids and moved them west to a 200-acre tract of land outside of Burnt River, Ontario. But like so many things human, the promises of the new happy way of life for the group was not long-lasting. Over the next year, things reverted to how it was before the child's death and prison for Theriault.

The following year brought the death of yet another child. This time a 5-month-old baby girl. After an autopsy, the death was ruled to be sudden infant death syndrome. But later, Lavallee testified that the baby died after Theriault ordered the newborn wrapped in a blanket and put out in a wheelbarrow for hours in the middle of the winter as punishment for crying.

In 1985, the Children's Aid Society was tipped off about many child abuse incidents occurring at Theriault's commune, and they staged a raid. Thirteen children were taken away from the commune during that raid and placed into foster care.

Over the following year, Dr. Martine Miljkovitch, an independent child abuse expert, evaluated eight of the children that had been removed from the commune. The children studied were from ages three to nine. Miljkovitch reported these children all assisted in births of babies, watched the adults participate in sex, and had sexual contact with each other.

Theriault demonstrated for them how the penis worked by masturbating in front of the children. He claimed that he did it as a form of education, and not for his satisfaction. After submitting her report to the court, Miljkovitch recommended that the children be allowed to return to the commune and back into the care of Theriault. Her report read,

> "There was a kind of naïve attitude that you have to expose children to these things because they are part of nature. Certainly, the children were allowed to have sexual activities among themselves, but the principles behind it weren't bad."

The court didn't agree with Dr. Miljkovitch and feared for the children's safety. They made all of the children they removed from the commune wards of the court. The children were placed with adoptive families unknown to any of the cult members.

On September 28, 1988, one of Theriault's spiritual wives, Solange Boilard, 32, complained of stomach pains. Theriault ordered Boilard placed, lying down, face up and naked on a wooden bakery table in their kitchen. A few minutes later, Theriault entered the room, wearing what could only be described as a holy costume, consisting of a long red robe, gold crown, and jewelry.

With a small group of his children watching, and his

nurse Lavallee by his side, Theriault was about to perform medical treatment on his spiritual wife. He started by winding his right arm back as far as he could, then releasing a hard punch into his wife's stomach. He then worked an enema tube up her rectum, and once he got the tube placed, poured olive oil and molasses into the tube.

Next, Theriault cut open his wife's abdomen, without anesthesia, and ripped out a piece of her intestines with his bare hand. He then turned to Lavallee, told her to stitch his wife back up, and left the room. Boilard died the next day, and they buried her on the commune.

Theriault became distraught over her death since not only was Boilard his spiritual wife, but she was also the bookkeeper for the cult's business. He dug up her body, had her cleaned up, took her back to his bedroom, where he cuddled with her, and told her how much he loved her.

The next day, she was again placed into a pine coffin and reburied. That evening, Theriault felt suicidal and grieved all night without getting any sleep. So, again the next day, he had her body dug up. Only this time, he cut a hole in her skull. According to Lavalle, he did this to masturbate into her skull. Then he buried her again. Theriault's process of digging up her body and performing some sort of ritual or operation on her lasted for more than a year. One time, he removed her ribs, split them up, and gave them to cult members to make necklaces. He then made them wear it.

In the summer of 1989, Theriault asked his harem of wives to each write a letter that praised him as a leader. Lavallee couldn't find it in her heart to write a letter of good things about him that she just didn't believe. She had grown to loathe him for all of the torture he put so many of the others through.

Theriault knew that he would have to punish her for this act of insubordination. So, when the two of them were in the kitchen, he stabbed her hand with a knife, hard enough to attach it to the kitchen table so she couldn't leave. For hours, he carved away at her arms, using a small carpet knife, deep enough in some places to reach the bone. At one point, she became so numb, suffering from severed tendons that she was convinced Theriault was finally going to kill her.

Theriault then dragged her outside and amputated her arm with an axe. Later, he had some of the other members try to stitch her arm back with twine and then cauterized the wound. Lavalle suffered tortures like these for three more weeks, until August 14, 1989, when she finally escaped through the woods to a nearby town, Burnt River.

Even though she was found weighing only 80 pounds, one arm severed, and clinging to life, Lavallee stayed loyal to Theriault. She refused to press charges or write a complaint about him. It was his legal wife, Gisele, who eventually told the stories to the welfare workers and police. A few weeks later, the police picked up Theriault on assault charges.

At the time of his arrest, Theriault didn't think the police knew anything about the murder of Boilard. He pleaded guilty on the assault charges of Lavallee. It took one more year for the police to get enough evidence to charge him with second-degree murder of Boilard, as well as assault for the disembowelment.

Theriault retained a good lawyer, Julian Falconer, who was plea bargaining for the murder charges to be lowered to manslaughter because Theriault was drunk at the time of the killing. However, Constable Robert Bowen of the Ontario Provincial Police diligently interviewed all of Theriault's victims and collected enough evidence to prove he was responsible for at least 84 assaults on his followers. When all of the attacks came to light, Theriault, pled guilty to the second-degree murder of Boilard, with the stipulation that none of the other assaults would be prosecuted. Theriault's evil and violent treatment of his followers would not be entered into the public record, but in 1993, he was still sentenced to life in prison.

Even though Theriault was in prison, he still managed to have children with three of his wives that stuck with him. Within one year of his being sent to prison, Francine Laflamme, 36, Chatal Labrie, 34, and Nicole Ruel, 35, moved into a log cabin located about a half-mile from the prison. Theriault was held at Millhaven Institute, a maximum-security prison in Kingston, Ontario. But life was still pretty sweet. In between Theriault writing his poems and creating his art, he had conjugal visits every six weeks with the wife of his choice. Theriault had now fathered 28 children.

Thirteen years into his sentence, Theriault came up for his first parole hearing. Although he initially made the application, when he got in front of the parole board, he decided that he wanted to withdraw his application. Theriault believed that his life would be in danger outside of the prison. After the hearing, they decided that he would be moved to a medium-maximum security prison, Dorchester

Penitentiary, in New Brunswick. He didn't want to leave the current prison that he was in since he had his life all set up to the way he liked it. But this was not his choice, and he had no say in the matter. The new prison was set up to handle drug and alcohol issues for prisoners, and Theriault was still dealing with those problems.

Shortly after his move into the new prison, on February 26, 2011, a convicted murderer Matthew Gerrard MacDonald walked into Theriault's cell and stabbed him in his neck with a shank, killing him almost instantly. The closed-circuit camera on Theriault's cell captured the bloody end to the 63-year-old cult leader, as MacDonald took his time slicing Theriault into pieces. MacDonald had never met Theriault before they were both in prison; in fact, they had never even encountered each other in prison. Instead, this was something that was in MacDonald's mind. He had watched several women throughout his own life tortured, beaten, raped, and even killed by men like Theriault. He confessed this to the correctional officers as they pulled him off Theriault's dead body.

Years later, Theriault was back in the news when his artwork was discovered on a website dedicated to murders called *murderauction.com*. In America, the Son of Sam law makes it nearly impossible for a criminal to profit from their crimes through books or television deals. But because Theriault was a Canadian, there are currently no restrictions on the sale of his items. Five pieces of Theriault's work appeared on the website for auction. After Theriault's death, his cell was cleaned out, and all items were left in a police warehouse.

At the time of this writing, the *Murder Auction website* had 17 items up for auction relating to Theriault. Among these items was an abstract Christmas 2007 oil painting by Theriault selling for $475, a green wooden beaded necklace selling for $5,500, and an abstract painting on stretched canvas with both hands in paint signed "Roch Moises Theriault" also from 2007.

III

CULTS METHODOLOGY AND HOW TO ESCAPE

"God told me to tell you...."

11

THE WASHING OF THE BRAIN

The study of brainwashing is often referred to as thought reform, which falls into the sphere of social influence. Social influence occurs every day, and in more ways now than ever before.

The advertising we are exposed to continually brainwashes us in some way, whether it's merely compliance, the "just do it" approach; persuasion, the "do it because it'll make you feel better" approach; or an educational method, the latest being the propaganda method, where you are told not to believe in what you've been taught. Brainwashing can use all of these methods to try and change the person's beliefs or change the way someone is thinking without that person's consent, or realization that it's happening.

Usually, we only hear about brainwashing occurring in prison camps or cults. Quite often, the brainwasher or agent uses methods to control the target's sleep patterns, eating, using the bathroom, and the fulfillment of any other basic human needs, until the target depends on the agent for everything. In the process, the agent systematically breaks down the target's identity to the point where it's no longer functioning correctly. Then the agent replaces the character with another set of behaviors, attitudes, and beliefs.

The steps involved in breaking down the 'self' are listed here:

1. **Assault on identity: "You are not who you think you are"** - This is a systematic attack on a target's sense of self (also called his identity or ego) and his core belief system. The agent denies everything that makes the target who he is: "You are not a soldier." "You are not a man." "You are not defending freedom." The target is under constant attack for days, weeks, or months, to the point that he becomes exhausted, confused, and disoriented. In this state, his beliefs seem less stable.
2. **Guilt: "You are bad"** - While the identity crisis is setting in, the agent is simultaneously creating an overwhelming sense of guilt in the target. He repeatedly and mercilessly attacks the subject for any 'sin' the target has committed, large or small. He may criticize the target for everything from the 'evilness' of his beliefs to the way he eats too slowly. The target begins to feel a general sense of shame, that everything he does is wrong.
3. **Self-betrayal: "Agree with me that you are bad"** - Once the subject is disoriented and drowning in guilt, the agent forces him to

denounce his family, friends, and peers who share the same 'wrong' belief system that he holds using threats of physical harm or continuance of mental attacks. The betrayal of his own beliefs and his people increases the shame and loss of identity the target is already experiencing.

4. **Breaking point: "Who am I? Where am I? And what am I supposed to do?"** - With his identity in crisis, experiencing deep shame, and having betrayed what he has always believed in, the target may undergo what in the lay community is referred to as a nervous breakdown. In psychology, a nervous breakdown is a collection of severe symptoms that can indicate any number of psychological disturbances. It may involve uncontrollable sobbing, deep depression, and general disorientation. The target may have lost his grip on reality and have the feeling of being completely lost and alone. When the target reaches his breaking point, his sense of self is pretty much up for grabs. He has no clear understanding of who he is or what is happening to him. At this point, the agent sets up the temptation to convert to another belief system that will save the target from his misery.

Many experts believe that even under ideal brainwashing conditions, the effects of the process are most often short-term. The victim's old identity is not, in fact, eradicated by the process, but instead, is in hiding. Once the 'replacement identity' stops being reinforced the person's old attitudes and beliefs should start to return.

Does the God or prophet that you believe in have to use deception or mind control? Do the ends justify the means? Would the world become the paradise that God wants it to be if the people following had no free will?

What do you think mind control is? Would it involve being taken into a dark cellar and tortured? Do you believe that you would know if you were under mind control right now? Mind control is just one aspect of a cult, but it is the hardest thing to realize about yourself, and then even harder to break away.

When a person leaves a cult, it disrupts their own identity, who they really are. They have lived for years inside a false identity that was given to them by the cult. The mind control becomes stronger each time someone from outside your cult tries to tell you that you've been brainwashed. It's something a follower believes is persecution and it's expected. They are told to expect it. Challenging it only makes their belief stronger.

To complete the brainwashing, the agent offers the possibility of salvation:

1. **Leniency: "I can help you**" - With the target in a state of crisis, the agent offers some small kindness or reprieve from the abuse. He may offer the target a drink of water or take a moment to ask the target what he misses about home. In a state of breakdown resulting from an endless psychological attack, any small kindness seems enormous, and the target may experience a sense of relief and gratitude

entirely out of proportion to the offering, even as if the agent has saved his life.

2. **Compulsion to confession: "You can help yourself"** - For the first time in the brainwashing process, the target experiences the contrast between the guilt and pain of identity assault and the sudden relief of leniency. The target may feel a desire to reciprocate the kindness offered to him, and at this point, the agent may present the possibility of confession as a means of relieving guilt and pain.
3. **Channeling of guilt: "This is why you're in pain**" - After weeks or months of assault, confusion, breakdown, and moments of leniency, the target's guilt has lost all meaning. He's not sure what he has done wrong; he just knows he is wrong. This confusion creates something of a blank slate that lets the agent fill in the blanks: He can attach that guilt, that sense of wrongness, to whatever he wants. The agent connects the target's guilt to the belief system the agent is trying to replace. The target comes to believe it is his belief system that is the cause of his shame. The contrast between old and new has been established: The old belief system is associated with psychological (and usually physical) agony, and the new belief system is associated with the possibility of escaping that agony.
4. **Releasing of guilt: "It's not me, it's my beliefs"** - The embattled target is relieved to

learn there is an external cause of his wrongness, that it is not he that is inescapably bad. An external cause means he can escape his wrongness by avoiding the wrong belief system. All he has to do is denounce the people and institutions associated with that belief system, and he won't be in pain anymore. The target has the power to release himself from the wrongness by confessing to acts associated with his old belief system. With his full confessions, the target has completed his psychological rejection of his former identity. It is now up to the agent to offer the target a new one.

12

CULT RECRUITMENT

You may have the idea that a typical "cult recruit" is a troubled young person, maybe with a mental illness, or someone who's easily exploited by unethical cultists. But studies show that people who join cults have only a slightly higher incidence of psychiatric disorders than the general population.

Cult members come from all walks of life, all age groups, and all personality types. However, one common thread among most cult recruits is heightened stress.

Research indicates that a majority of people who end up joining a cult were recruited during a particularly stressful period in their lives, such as the stress associated with adolescence, leaving home for the first time, a bad breakup, losing a job, or the death of a loved one. People undergoing significant stress can be more vulnerable, thereby susceptible when a person or group claims to have the answer to all of their problems.

Michael Langone, Ph.D., a psychologist who specializes in cults, also identifies some psychological traits that can make a person more likely to be successfully recruited:

- Dependency - an intense desire to belong, stemming from a lack of self-confidence,
- Desire for spiritual meaning - a need to believe that life has a "higher purpose,"
- Disillusionment with the status quo - a feeling of marginalization within one's own culture and a desire to see that culture change,
- Gullibility - a tendency to believe what someone says without really thinking about it,
- Low tolerance for uncertainty - a need to have any question answered immediately in black-and-white terms,
- Naive idealism - a blind belief that everyone is good,
- Unassertiveness - a reluctance to say no or question authority.

Cult recruiters hang out in places where you might find people in a period of extreme stress or possessing the above personality traits, which is truthfully anywhere. Some particularly fruitful recruiting locations for cultists include college campuses, religious gatherings, self-help and support groups, seminars and conferences relating to spirituality or social change, and the unemployment office.

In a 1990 article in the San Francisco Examiner, an unnamed ex-cult member commented on how easy it was to get sucked in:

> "People don't realize how susceptible we all are. Those smiling faces lead you to buy it when you're naive and accepting."

She was recruited on the UC San Diego campus when she was 19 years old. Her parents arranged for her to be 'deprogrammed' eight years later (more on deprogramming in the "Getting Out" chapter).

The main methods of cult recruitment revolve around deception and manipulation. Potential recruits are not told the true nature or intentions of the group. Instead, recruiters portray what they are selling as something mainstream, low-pressure, and harmless. They might tell people at a church gathering that their group meets once a week to brainstorm ways to raise money for a new homeless shelter. Or, they might invite a high school student to a lecture about how public service can enhance a college application.

Recruiters identify the specific needs or desires of their targets and play to them. They learn to pick up on a person's fears and vulnerabilities and portray the cult accordingly. For instance, if a young woman just went through a bad breakup, and she's feeling depressed and alone, a cult member might tell her that his group helps people to overcome interpersonal problems and rebuild their confidence for a fresh start. If a man just lost his wife in a car accident, and he can't bear that he didn't get to say goodbye to her, a recruiter might claim that his group helps people reach peace in the wake of sudden death.

It might seem strange that someone would accept these

types of invitations, but there are a couple of factors that make it look more palatable. First, the recruiter might be someone these people know. He could be in that young woman's college dorm or that man's survivor support group. And someone sad, lonely, or desperate might be more inclined to trust someone who claims to know the path back to happiness.

Also, cults typically isolate recruits, so they don't have an opportunity to get a reality check from friends or family. They might hold meetings or services at times that usually would be spent with family and friends; they might hold retreats that submerge the recruit in the group's message for days at a time; or they might ask recruits not to discuss the group with others until they know more about it, so they don't mislead people or give them only part of the story.

This kind of isolation narrows a person's feedback structure drastically for some time, to the point that the only people they're communicating with are the members of the cult they're being invited to join. Their doubts about the group, therefore, are never reinforced, and they end up turning into self-doubt, instead. Looking around them at all of the smiling, friendly people who have found peace and happiness by following this path, it appears that it must be the right way.

Once a person attends one meeting, service, or lecture, he's invited to another, and another, and another. He's welcomed into the cult family and encouraged to commit himself to the group. From day one, it's a process of manipulation and deception. And for those who stick around, the recruiting process culminates in the submission of their personalities to the 'will of the group.'

13

CULT INDOCTRINATION

A destructive cult uses many techniques to get its members to stay, commit themselves, and take part in what may be harmful activities. The sum of these techniques constitutes what some people call "mind control." It's also known as "thought reform," "brainwashing," and "coercive persuasion," and it involves the systematic breakdown of a person's sense of self.

Patty Hearst, the heiress to the Hearst publishing fortune, became famous in the 1970s after she was kidnapped by the Symbionese Liberation Army (SLA), which some deemed to be a political cult, and allegedly brainwashed her into joining the group. There are reports that Hearst was locked in a dark closet for several days after her kidnapping and was kept hungry, tired, brutalized, and afraid for her life while SLA members bombarded her with their anti-capitalist political ideology.

Within two months of her kidnapping, Patty had changed her name, issued a statement in which she referred to her family as the "pig-Hearsts," and appeared on a security tape robbing a bank with her kidnappers.

Thought reform is an umbrella term for any number of manipulative techniques used to get people to do something they wouldn't otherwise do. The concept of thought reform itself is a controversial one. Some say its mere propaganda designed to scare people away from new religions and political movements. But most psychologists believe that cult brainwashing techniques, which are similar to techniques used in prisoner interrogation, do change a person's thought processes.

In cult recruiting and indoctrination, many brainwashing techniques are used:

Deception

Cults trick recruits into joining the group and committing themselves to a cause or lifestyle they don't fully understand. Cults and their leaders may:

- mislead recruits/members as to the real expectations and activities of the group;
- hide any signs of illegal, immoral, or hyper-controlling practices until the recruit has fully immersed himself in the group;
- use a member's altered consciousness, induced by activities like meditation, chanting, or drug use, to increase vulnerability to suggestion.

Isolation

Cults cut off members from the outside world (and

even each other) to produce intense introspection, confusion, loss of perspective, and a distorted sense of reality. The members of the cult become the person's only social contact and feedback mechanism. Cults and their leaders may:

- keep recruits from talking to other recruits. They may only be allowed to speak with long-committed members for a while;
- disallow unsupervised contact with the outside world. In this way, there is no chance for a reality check or validation of a new member's concerns regarding the group;
- instill the belief that outsiders (non-cult members) are dangerous and wrong.

Induce Dependency

Cults demand absolute and unquestioning, devotion, loyalty, and submission. A cult member's sense of self is systematically destroyed. Ultimately, feelings of worthlessness and evil become associated with independence and critical thinking, and feelings of warmth and love become associated with unquestioning submission. Cults and their leaders may:

- Control every minute of a member's waking time so there is no free time to think or analyze;
- Remove members from all decision-making. They are told what to eat, what to wear, how to feed their children, when to sleep, etc.;
- Devalue and criticize any special talents the

member has to confuse the member's sense of self-worth;

- Punish the member for any doubts, assertiveness, or having remaining ties to the outside world. Punishment by the group will be in the form of criticism, guilt, and alienation. Questions and doubts are systematically turned around so that the doubter feels wrong, worthless, and evil for questioning. The member is loved again when he renounces those doubts and submits to the will of the leader;
- Deprive the member of adequate sustenance and/or sleep, so the mind becomes muddled;
- Alternate praise and love with scorn and punishment randomly to keep the member off-balance, confused, and to instil immense self-doubt. The leader may offer occasional gifts and special privileges to encourage continued submission;
- Pressure the member to confess sins publicly, after which the group viciously ridicules him for being evil and unworthy. He is loved again when he acknowledges that his devotion to the cult is the only thing that will bring him salvation.

Dread

Once complete dependence is established, the member must retain the leader's good favor, or else his life falls apart. Cults and their leaders may:

- Punish doubt or insubordination with physical or emotional trauma;
- Ensure the member feels like his only family is the group, and he has nowhere else to go. This is accomplished by ensuring all ties to the outside world have been cut;
- Control access to necessities. The member must behave, or he may not get food, water, social interaction, or protection from the outside world. Access depends on the leader's favor;
- Make the member believe that only group members are "saved." So if he leaves, he will face eternal damnation.

Indoctrination, or thought reform, is a long process that never really ends. Members are continually subjected to these techniques; it's part of daily life in a cult. Some adjust well to it after a while, embracing their new role as group member and casting aside their old sense of independence. For others, it's a perpetually stressful existence.

CULT LIFE (AND DEATH)

There is no single description that fits the lifestyle of every destructive cult out there. But there are some common themes. Many ex-cult members depict a type of insulated, moment-to-moment existence in which repressing fear and anxiety is most important. Chanting and meditation become prime coping mechanisms in this regard. Cut off from family, old friends, and the outside world, their old life becomes like a dream. In their new life, psychological growth stops. Cult members are caught in a static life that depends on not thinking, not questioning, not wondering, not remembering. Children raised in a destructive cult are stunted early. They do not usually attend school, and the cult may or may not provide its children with an education.

Cults need food, shelter, and clothing like everyone else, and unless they have a wealthy benefactor or are isolated and living somewhere they can grow their food, that means they need money. Some cults make money to sustain themselves by legitimate means. As discussed above, The Heaven's Gate cult in San Diego, California, ran a successful website design business before they committed mass suicide in 1997. Some cults commit crimes like fraud and tax evasion to help support themselves. They may use deceptive fundraising techniques or require recruits to make significant financial contributions to support the rest of the cult.

Above all else, life in a totalism cult is typically characterized by tight control. There is very little freedom in daily life: The leader prescribes what a member can and cannot do for every minute of the day, including what food he can eat, what books he can read, whom he can talk to, what he can wear, where he can go, and how long he can sleep. The leader makes decisions, and the followers do as they're told.

For some people, living this way is a relief. Life is simple. There are no unanswered questions, no uncertainty, no worrying about the future, or managing conflicting desires. Some people's lives on the outside were so bad that the cult is, in reality, a safe and happy place. But in a lot of cases, this type of lifestyle causes intense psychological distress. Many people experience a persistent fear of angering the leader or losing group approval. They must continuously avoid the tension between their cult world and their former life and stifle any doubts or longings that arise.

In some cases, there is also the possibility of physical harm. Punishments for disobedience might be physical, and cult members are typically cut off from hospitals and regular medical care. Some studies show that children in destructive cults are more likely to be abused or neglected than in the general population.

This level of stress can lead to chronic anxiety, physical illness, or even a complete mental breakdown in which a cult member may become unable to function in daily life. It's the people who experience cult life as stressful who are most likely to leave voluntarily.

14

ESCAPING THE CULT

People voluntarily leave a cult for any number of reasons. Some cult members become disillusioned and walk out, as was the case with the Davidians, the precursor group to the Branch Davidians discussed previously. The leader of the Davidians predicted the end of the world on a particular date. When that date came and went, some members were disappointed. The leader predicted a new date, and that date came and went as well with the world still intact. By the time the leader died, and his wife took over and predicted a new series of dates, and again that failed to see the destruction of the world, there were very few members left in the group.

For some people, it's not that difficult to leave a cult. Some individuals are just less susceptible to mind-control techniques than others, and they may have retained enough of a sense of self to make an informed decision to walk out.

But for most, it's usually not that simple. Some excultists say they spent years working up the nerve to get out. A true convert is utterly dependent on the cult for every aspect of life and consciousness. To the truly indoctrinated cult member, leaving the cult means being alone and starting over. His sense of self has been completely broken down to the point that he doesn't even know who he is without his cult family. He may not have made a single decision in years.

Gathering the confidence to leave a totalism cult voluntarily requires a tremendous act of will and doesn't come easily. It might result from renewed contact with the outside world, such as a cult member speaking with her parents for the first time in a decade. It might happen when a cult member has a psychological breakdown and believes she is too worthless to meet the expectations of the group, so she leaves to spare her cult family the weariness of her presence. Or it might come about following a particularly traumatic experience that jolts the cult member into consciousness, such as witnessing the sexual assault of a child or a murder within the cult.

But deciding to leave is only part of the process. The cult has to unlock the door, so to speak, for the member to get out.

Some destructive cults do let people leave. Usually, they'll put a lot of pressure on a member to stay; but in the end, a person can choose to go and not have to climb a barbed-wire fence in the dead of night or sneak past armed guards. In the mildest cases, a member who leaves may be disowned by the cult, forbidden any contact with the people that have been her family for months, years, or decades, but the member won't suffer any physical harm when she walks out.

In the most severe cases, though, a cult may stop at nothing to maintain control over its members, and a person has to fear for her life if she tries to leave. As mentioned above, when 16 members of The People's Temple in Jonestown, Guyana, decided they wanted to leave the cult, several armed cult members followed them to the airport and opened fire.

While a peaceful, voluntary exit is undoubtedly the preferred method of leaving a cult, it doesn't always happen that way. There are also those who may not want to escape at all but are snatched from their beds at three in the morning and dragged back into the outside world. This ‘snatch and grab’ is the first stage in what is known as "deprogramming," an extreme method of removing someone from a cult against his will.

It's not easy to get someone to leave a destructive cult. Talking is always the first step. But sometimes, the cultist is too deeply indoctrinated to hear anything an outsider has to say. Other times, there's no opportunity to talk at all. A cult member may have severed all ties to the outside world. Family members who fear for a loved one who's deeply involved in a totalistic cult have to find another option if simple talking is impossible or doesn't work. At this point, they can go one of two ways: deprogramming or exit counseling.

CULT DEPROGRAMMING

Deprogramming is the more drastic of the two approaches because it usually involves an initial kidnapping to get the cult member away from the cult. Because of its extreme and risky nature, deprogramming is a very expensive service. It can cost in the tens of thousands of dollars. After the forced removal, deprogramming involves hours and hours of intense "debriefing," during which a team of deprogrammers hold the cult member against his will and use ethical psychological techniques to try to counter the unethical psychological techniques used by the cult. The goal is to get the cult member to think for himself and re-evaluate his situation. Debriefing methods can include

- Educating the cult member on thought-reform techniques and helping him to recognize those methods in his own cult experience;
- Asking questions that encourage the cult member to think in a critical, independent way, helping him to recognize that type of thinking and praising him for it;
- Attempting to produce an emotional connection to his former life by introducing objects from his past and having family members share their memories of his pre-cult existence.

Deprogramming was relatively common in the 1970s but has fallen out of favor as an acceptable cult-removal method – partly because it's so expensive and partly because it involves kidnapping and imprisonment that could potentially lead to a lawsuits.

CULT EXIT COUNSELING

Today, most families turn to exit counselors. Exit counseling leaves out the kidnapping and focuses instead on employing psychological techniques that might get the cult member to submit to debriefing voluntarily.

Exit counselors guide the family in the most effective ways to get a cult member to communicate with outsiders. Family members must be nonjudgmental, calm, and loving, or else they'll only reinforce the belief that all outsiders are harmful and dangerous. If they succeed, and the cult member agrees to participate in the process, what happens next is essentially the same debriefing that occurs during deprogramming – long sessions that take place over many days, but the cult member is free to leave.

There is no guarantee that any cult-removal technique will work. Some sources say that at least one-third of the deprogramming method fails, and there are no definitive statistics yet on the success rate of exit counseling. But when it does work, the cult member finds himself back in the outside world with a whole new set of problems.

People who leave a totalistic cult can suffer from a laundry list of psychological problems, including depression, anxiety, paranoia, guilt, rage, and constant fear. They may have difficulty thinking clearly, making decisions, analyzing situations, and performing everyday activities like picking out something to wear or going to the store to buy groceries.

Psychologist Michael Langone describes a common post-cult state he calls "floating," in which the former member goes back and forth from "cult to non-cult ways of viewing the world, stalled in a foggy, 'in-between' state of consciousness."

Not everyone is psychologically damaged by having a cult experience. Some go on with life after a relatively short adjustment period. But most people who have undergone thought reform suffer negative consequences when they leave the insulated environment of the cult. It can take years for a former cult member to readjust to life on the outside. Some people never entirely return to their pre-cult level of functioning. But in most cases, counseling and family support can go a long way toward recovery.

ACKNOWLEDGMENTS

I would like to recognize the exceptional contribution from those who were once in or are still in, one of the cults discussed in this book. It takes an unimaginable amount of bravery to come forward and expose yourself to a not always sympathetic public. Your courage is one of the main reasons I was able to write this book with the comprehension I did. I could not have possibly done it without you. I hope that you find peace in your life.

A special thank you to my family, who stuck with me as I traveled all the winding roads to find the details of this story. Some of those roads included the darkest aspects of human history.

To the publishing team that supported me through my endeavor, cover designer, proof-readers, and editors who gave it their all to make this book the best it could be, thank you!

ABOUT THE AUTHOR

Alan R. Warren has written several Best-Selling True Crime books and has been one of the hosts and producer of the popular NBC news talk radio show ***House of Mystery*** which reviews True Crime, History, Science, Religion, Paranormal mysteries that we live with every day. From a darker, comedic and logical perspective, he has interviewed guests such as Robert Kennedy Jr., F. Lee Bailey, Aphrodite Jones, Marcia Clark, Nancy Grace, Dan Abrams and Jesse Ventura. The show is based in Seattle on KKNW 1150 AM and syndicated on the NBC network throughout the United States including on KCAA 106.5 FM Los Angeles/Riverside/Palm Springs, as well in Utah, New Mexico, and Arizona.

ALSO BY ALAN R. WARREN

BEYOND SUSPICION RUSSELL WILLIAMS: A CANADIAN SERIAL KILLER

#1 Bestselling Book in True Crime

Young girl's panties started to go missing; sexual assaults began to occur, and then female bodies were found! Soon this quiet town of Tweed, Ontario, was in panic. What's even more shocking was when an upstanding resident stood accused of the assaults. This was not just any man, but a pillar of the community; a decorated military pilot who had flown Canadian Forces VIP aircraft for dignitaries such as the Queen of England,

Prince Philip, the Governor General and the Prime Minister of Canada.

This is the story of serial killer Russell Williams, the elite pilot of Canada's Air Force One, and the innocent victims he murdered. Unlike other serial killers, Williams seemed very unaffected about his crimes and leading two different lives.

Alan R. Warren describes the secret life including the abductions, rape and murders that were unleashed on an unsuspecting community. Included are letters written to the victims by Williams and descriptions of the assaults and rapes as seen on videos and photos taken by Williams during the attacks.

This updated version also contains the full brilliant police interrogation of Williams and his confession, and the twisted way in which Williams planned to pin his crimes on his unsuspecting neighbor.

DEADLY BETRAYAL: THE TRUE STORY OF JENNIFER PAN - DAUGHTER FROM HELL

Find out what really happened when seasoned true crime reporter and author, Alan R. Warren, takes you through the details as they unfold in this book of a Deadly Betrayal.

A family of three tied up, each with a gun to their head. "Where's the money? Where's the fucking money?" one of the intruders yelled. A petrified daughter tortured and forced to listen to her parents being shot in cold blood. "I heard shots, like pops," she told the 911 operator, "somebody's broke into our home, please, I need help!" Was this a home invasion? Or something else, more sinister, a Deadly Betrayal.

The real-life horror story that happened inside the Pan family home shocked their normally peaceful upscale Toronto neighborhood. The Pans were an example of an immigrant family. Hann and his wife, Bich Pan, fled from Vietnam to Canada after the U.S.-Vietnamese war to find a better life. Their daughter, Jennifer, was an Olympic-caliber figure skater, an award-winning pianist, and a straight A student.

The Pans worked their way up in this rags-to-riches story, now living in a beautiful home with luxury cars in the driveway. Was it these expensive items that lured three intruders with guns into their home on the night of November 8, 2010?

REFERENCES

1. The Family International website, Our History, https://www.thefamilyinternational.org/en/about/ourhistory/
2. Novak J., Steven: *LSD before Leary: Sidney Cohen's Critique of 1950s Psychedelic Drug Research*, Isis, Vol. 88, No. 1, pp. 87-110.
3. Maclean, J.R.; Macdonald, D.C.; Ogden, F.; Wilby, E., *LSD25 and mescaline as therapeutic adjuvants*.
4. Abramson, H., Ed., *The Use of LSD in Psychotherapy and Alcoholism,* Bobbs-Merrill: New York, 1967, pp. 407–426.
5. Ditman, K.S.; Bailey, J.J., *Evaluating LSD as a psychotherapeutic agent*, pp.74–80.
6. Hoffer, A., *A program for the treatment of alcoholism: LSD, malvaria, and nicotinic acid*, pp. 353–402.
7. United States. Congress. House. Committee on Interstate and Foreign Commerce. Subcommittee on Public Health and Welfare

(1968). Increased controls over hallucinogens and other dangerous drugs: hearings before the Subcommittee on Public Health and Welfare of the Committee on Interstate and Foreign Commerce, House of Representatives, Ninetieth Congress, second session, on H.R. 14096, a bill to amend the Federal food, drug, and cosmetic act to prescribe penalties for the possession of LSD and other hallucinogenic drugs by unauthorized persons, [and] H.R. 15355, a bill to amend the Federal food, drug, and cosmetic act by increasing the penalties for illegal manufacture and traffic in hallucinogenic drugs (including LSD) and other depressant and stimulant drugs, including possession of such drugs for sale or other disposal to another, and by making it a misdemeanor to possess any such drug for one's own use except when prescribed or furnished by a licensed practitioner, and for other purposes (and similar bills). Washington: U.S. Govt. Print. Off. Retrieved 14 October 2016.

8. *Project MKUltra, the Central Intelligence Agency's Program of Research into Behavioral Modification* (PDF). U.S. Government Printing Office (copy hosted at the New York Times website). August 8, 1977. Retrieved 2010-04-18.
9. ACHRE Report, *Chapter 3: Supreme Court Dissents Invoke the Nuremberg Code: CIA and DOD Human Subjects Research Scandals,* Archived from the original on 2013-03-31,

Retrieved 2012-11-08. Archived 2013-03-31 at the Wayback Machine.

10. *U.S. Senate Report on CIA MKULTRA Behavioral Modification Program 1977 - Public Intelligence,* publicintelligence.net.
11. United States Senate, 95th Congress, 1st session (3 August 1977). *Project MKUltra, The CIA's Program of Research in Behavioral Modification (PDF).* Joint Hearing Before the Select Committee on Intelligence and the Subcommittee on Health and Scientific Research of the Committee on Human Resources (Report).
12. O'Neill, Tom: *Chaos*, Little, Brown and Company, Kindle Edition, p. 308.
13. Sanders, Ed: *The Family*, 2002, Da Capo Press, p. 407.
14. Jensen, Vickie (2011): *Women Criminals: An Encyclopedia of People and Issues*, ABC-CLIO, p. 293, ISBN 0313337136
15. Fox, Margalit (2009-09-26): *Susan Atkins, Manson Follower, Dies at 61,* The New York Times.Retrieved 2009-09-26.
16. Deutsch, Linda (2009-09-25): *Charles Manson follower Susan Atkins dies,* Associated Press, archived from the original on 2009-09-28.
17. Woo, Elaine (September 26, 2009): *Susan Atkins dies at 61; imprisoned Charles Manson follower,* Los Angeles Times, retrieved November 15, 2012.
18. Fromme, Lynette (2018): *Reflexion*, The Peasenhall Press, ISBN 978-0-9913725-1-5.

19. User, Super: *The Charles Manson (Tate-LaBianca Murder) Trial: The Defendants,* www.famous-trials.com, retrieved 2018-09-24.
20. https://www.biography.com/people/patricia-krenwinkel20902495
21. Atkins, Susan (1977): *Child of Satan, Child of God: Her own story,* Logos International, p. 175, *ISBN 0882702297.*
22. Los Angeles Times: *Manson follower Leslie Van Houten granted parole in notorious murders,* retrieved October 10, 2017.
23. *Leslie Van Houten, Ex-Manson Follower, Approved for Parole,* NBC News, New York City, September 7, 2017.
24. Bugliosi, Vincent; Gentry, Curt (1974): *Helter Skelter,* Arrow Books Limited, ISBN 0-09-997500-9.
25. Winn, Denise: *The Manipulated Mind: Brainwashing, Conditioning, and Indoctrination*, p168.
26. Hall Mears, Hadley: *The Story of the Abandoned Movie Ranch Where the Manson Family Launched Helter Skelter,* Cult Education Institute, retrieved 18/12/14, Curbed, Los Angeles, October 22, 2014.
27. Senate Government Affairs Permanent Subcommittee on Investigations, October 31, 1995: *Global Proliferation of Weapons of Mass Destruction: A Case Study on the Aum Shinrikyo,* Federation of American Scientists, FAS.org., retrieved 24 December 2015.
28. Ramzy, Austin: *Japan Executes Cult Leader*

Behind 1995 Sarin Gas Subway Attack, The New York Times, 5 July 2018.

29. BBC News: *Tokyo Sarin attack: Aum Shinrikyo cult leaders executed, 6 July 2018, retrieved 12 July 2018.*
30. RT.COM: *Russia bans murderous Japanese sect Aum Shinrikyo as terrorist group,* accessed 12 July 2018.
31. Danzig, Richard; Sageman, Marc; Leighton, Terrance; Hough, Lloyd; Yuki, Hidemi; Kotani, Rui; Hosford, Zachary M, (2000), *Aum Shinrikyo Insights into How Terrorists Develop Biological and Chemical Weapons (PDF). Center for a New American Security.* p. 10. Archived from the original (PDF) on 16 March 2016. Retrieved 14 May 2015.
32. Griffith, Lee (2004): *The War on Terrorism and the Terror of God,* William B. Eerdmans Publishing Company, *p. 164,* ISBN: 978-0-8028-2860-6.
33. Goldwag, Arthur (2009): *Cults, Conspiracies, and Secret Societies: The Straight Scoop on Freemasons, the Illuminati, Skull and Bones, Black Helicopters, the New World Order, and Many, Many More,* Random House, p.15, ISBN: 978-0-307-39067-7.
34. The Japan Times Online: *Profiles of top Aum Shinrikyo members, including six still on death row, 10 July 2018, retrieved 10 July 2018.*
35. BBC News: *Last Aum cult fugitive Katsuya Takahashi arrested in Japan,* 15 June 2012, retrieved 18 January 2014.

36. BBC News: *Japanese police raid cult offices, 16 September 2006, retrieved 25 April 2010.*
37. Japan Times: *Surveillance of Aum to continue on grounds it still poses threat to public, Retrieved 2 January 2012.*
38. Japan Today: *9 injured as man rams car into pedestrians in Harajuku in retaliation for execution, 1 January 2019, retrieved 1 January 2019.*
39. BBC News: *Cult members die in 'mass suicide, retrieved 19 November 2019.*
40. *BBC News: Conductor cleared of cult deaths, December 20, 2006, retrieved May 20, 2010.*
41. Religion News Blog: *Conductor on trial over cult killings in France, Switzerland and Canada, 25 October 2006, retrieved 23 August 2017.*
42. Galanter, Marc: *Cults: Faith, Healing, and Coercion*, New York: Oxford University Press, 1989.
43. Davis, Eric: *Solar Temple Pilots,* The Village Voice, October 25, 1994.
44. Hassan-Gordon, Tariq: *Solar Temple Cult Influenced by Ancient Egypt,* Middle East Times, Issue 18, 2001.
45. Gordon, Sean: *Trial highlights Canadian cult link,* Toronto Star, 25 October 2006, p. A3, retrieved 2006 10-25.
46. *Musician Denies Solar Temple Murders,* The Scotsman, Edinburgh, April 18, 2001.
47. *Spanish cops arrest cult leader,* Associated Press, January 8, 1998.

48. James R. Lewis (editor): *The Order of the Solar Temple: The Temple of Death*, Ashgate Publishing Company, Ashgate Controversial New Religions Series, 2006, ISBN: 0-7546-5285-8.
49. CNN: *Heaven's Gate suicides remembered,* March 25, 2011, retrieved 2019-06-01.
50. Cornwell, Tim: *Heaven's Gate member found dead,* 7 May 1997, The Independent, retrieved 23 June 2014.
51. Stanziano, Don: *Cult Inspires First Copycat Suicide,* April 2, 1997, North County Times, pp. A-4, retrieved December 2, 2019.
52. The San Diego Union-Tribune: *Heaven's Gate: A timeline,* 18 March 2007, Archived from the original on 2008-10-03, retrieved 2007-10-21.
53. *Last Chance to Evacuate Earth Before Its Recycled, www.heavensgate.com, retrieved 2019-05-26.*
54. Ross, Rick: *Heaven's Gate' Suicides,* October 1999, The Rick A. Ross Institute.
55. Kube, Michelle: *March 26, 1997 - - Heaven's Gate Suicides,* March 27, 2017, kfiam640. iheart.com, retrieved June 3, 2019.
56. Zeller, Benjamin E.: *Heaven's Gate: America's UFO Religion,* NYU Press, 2014, ISBN: 1-4798-0381-2.
57. The General Association of Branch Davidian Seventh Day Adventists: *The Shepherd's Rod, Vol. 1,* thebranch.org, retrieved 2011-03-18.
58. PBS Frontline: *Biography: David Koresh, retrieved 21 May 2016.*

59. Pitts, William L.: *Davidians and Branch Davidians,* Handbook of Texas – Texas State Historical Association. Retrieved November 25, 2012.
60. http://www.dailymail.co.uk/news/article-2588106/Wewerent-brainwashed-Waco-cult-survivor-claims-newmemoir-Branch-Davidian-leader-David-Koresh-19-wivesslept-girls-young-12.htmlh.
61. The General Association of Branch Davidians.
62. Mitchell, Douglas: *Waco Untold, How David Koresh Stole the Identity of The Branch Davidians,* 2018, Ten Strings Publishing, ISBN 978-0-9998026-0-1.
63. Wright, Stuart A.: *Armageddon in Waco: Critical Perspectives on the Branch Davidian Conflict*, p.22.
64. Burnett, John: *Two Decades Later, Some Branch Davidians Still Believe,* April 20, 2013, National Public Radio, retrieved 12 May 2016.
65. The Associated Press: *Near Waco, a New Fight Over an Old Compound,* New York Times, retrieved 12 May 2016.
66. Neil Rawles: *Inside Waco* (Television documentary). February 2, 2007, Channel 4/HBO.
67. FBI: *"Report to the Deputy Attorney General on the Events at Waco, Texas/Child Abuse".*
68. Gazecki, William; Gifford, Dan; McNulty, Michael: *Waco: The Rules of Engagement,* 1997, Film Documentary, retrieved 25 November 2012.

69. Lubbock Avalanche-Journal/Associated Press: *Vampire cult town shrinks under national spotlight,* December 2, 1996.
70. Court TV: *Florida v. Rod Ferrell - The Vampire Cult Slaying Case,* June 22, 2001.
71. Jones, Aphrodite: *The Embrace: A True Vampire Story*, June 1, 2000, ISBN: 0-671-03467-7.
72. Seigenthaler, John: *MSNBC Investigates*, MSNBC, October 26, 2002.
73. Watson, Charles: *About Charles,* Aboundinglove.org, *Abounding Love Ministries, retrieved 25 February 2016.*
74. Parole Board Hearing Transcript 2011.
75. Hamilton, Matt: *Parole denied for convicted Manson follower Charles 'Tex' Watson,* MSN, Archived from the original on 2017-04-08, retrieved 201610-28.
76. Watson, Charles: *Will You Die for Me,* Abounding Love Ministries, p. 96, retrieved July 13, 2019.
77. Linder, Doug(2014): *The Charles Manson (Tate–LaBianca Murder) Trial,* University of Missouri–Kansas City School of Law. Archived from the original on 3 March 2016.
78. http://www.aboundinglove.org/main/
79. Cooper, Paulette: *The Scandal Behind the "Scandal of Scientology,"* www.cs.cmu.edu., retrieved November 8, 2019.
80. Goodsell, Greg: *Manson once proclaimed Scientology,* Catholic Online, February 23, 2010, www.catholic.org., archived from the

original on February 27, 2010, retrieved February 24, 2010.

81. Los Angeles Times: *Charles Manson Quickly Denied Parole,* April 11, 2012, Archived from the original on April 11, 2012, retrieved April 11, 2012.
82. *Biderman's Chart of Coercion*, reFOCUS, http://www.refocus.org/coerchrt.html.
83. *Characteristics of a Destructive Cult*, International Cultic Studies Association, http://www.csj.org/infoserv_articles/refocus.htm.
84. *Cults*, WorkingPsychology Website. http://www.workingpsychology.com/cult.html.
85. *Cults: a.k.a. New Religious Movements*, ReligiousTolerance.org, http://www.religioustolerance.org/cultintro.htm.
86. Enroth, Ronald, Ph.D: *Dysfunctional Churches*, Cult Observer, 1992, Vol. 9, No. 4. http://www.csj.org/infoserv_articles/enroth_ronald_dysfunctional_churches.htm.
87. Groenveld, Jan: *Identifying a Cult,* ex-cult Resource Center, http://www.ex-cult.org/General/identifying-a-cult.
88. Hassan, Steven: *Mind Control - The BITE Model*, ex-cult Resource Center, http://www.ex-cult.org/bite.html.
89. Irving, Carl: *One who got away: Cult recruiting flourishing quietly on college campuses*, San Francisco Examiner, March 4, 1990, http://www.rickross.com/reference/srichinmoy/srichinmoy13.html.
90. *Destructive Cults: The Family (Charles*

Manson), ReligiousTolerance.org. http://www.religioustolerance.org/dc_charl.htm.

91. PBS: *Guerrilla: The Taking of Patty Hearst*, American Experience, PBS.org. http://www.pbs.org/wgbh/amex/guerrilla/peopleevents/p_p_hearst.html.
92. Jacobsen, Jeff: *A Short Review of Academic Research into Cults*, ex-cult Resource Center, http://www.excult.org/General/review.academic.research
93. Langone, Michael D., Ph.D: *Cults: Questions and Answers,* International Cultic Studies Association, http://www.csj.org/infoserv_articles/langone_michael_cultsqa.htm.
94. Lifton, Robert J., Ph.D: *Thought Reform: The Psychology of Totalism*, ex-cult Resource Center, http://www.excult.org/General/lifton-criteria
95. *The People's Temple,* Religious Tolerance.org, http://www.religioustolerance.org/dc_jones.htm 97.
96. Rosedale, Herbert H., Esq. and Michael D. Langone, Ph.D: *On Using the Term 'Cult',* International Cultic Studies Association, http://www.csj.org/infoserv_articles/langone_michael_term_cult.htm.
97. Ryan, Patrick: *Mass Suicides Timeline*, International Cultic Studies Association, http://www.csj.org/infoserv_articles/ryan_patrick_suicide_timeline.htm.
98. Singer, Margaret T., Ph. D: *Conditions for Mind Control*, ex-cult Resource Center,

http://www.excult.org/General/singer-conditions.

99. Troy, Carol: *Behind Suicide Cult Lay Thriving Web Business,* The New York Times, Mar. 28, 1997. http://partners.nytimes.com/library/cyber/week/032897cult.h

100. PBS: *Waco: The Inside Story*, PBS.org. http://www.pbs.org/wgbh/pages/frontline/waco/topten.html.

101. https://english.religion.info/2003/06/12/ourterrestrial-journey-is-coming-to-an-end-the-last-voyageof-the-solar-temple/

102. San Diego State University: Jonestown Project, *What happened to Peoples Temple after 18 November 1978?,* Alternative Considerations of Jonestown and Peoples Temple.

www.ingramcontent.com/pod-product-compliance
Lightning Source LLC
Chambersburg PA
CBHW071812080526
44589CB00012B/764
9781777259402